MARK

"I have taught Jeff Brantley's mindfulness techniques to my DBT class and their hope is renewed—my clients have raved that simply focusing on their breath and learning these skills has been life changing. This is a must read for anyone who has struggled with anxiety."

—Sarah Faber Cameron, MA, LPA,
psychotherapist, Durham, NC

"I would not hesitate to recommend this book to my clients. The importance of the mind/body connection and its relation to health and well-being comes through loud and clear. Anyone suffering the misery of anxiety, fear, or panic will find an excellent road map toward healing and wellness through the practice of mindfulness and by 'connecting with what is here and holding it in kind and compassionate awareness.'"

—Mark Wolever, Ph.D., Licensed
Psychologist and President of Health
Psychology Associates, Inc., Durham NC.

calming your anxious mind

how mindfulness and compassion can free you from anxiety, fear, and panic

JEFFREY BRANTLEY, MD

Foreword by JON KABAT-ZINN, PH.D.

New Harbinger Publications, Inc.

Publisher's Note

This publication is designed to provide accurate and authoritative informa-
tion in regard to the subject matter covered. It is sold with the understanding
that the publisher is not engaged in rendering psychological, financial,
legal, or other professional services. If expert assistance or counseling is
needed, the services of a competent professional should be sought.

Distributed in Canada by Raincoast Books

New Harbinger Publications, Inc.
5674 Shattuck Avenue
Oakland, CA 94609

"I Give You Back" on page 201 is from the book *She Had Some Horses* by
Joy Harjo. Copyright © 1983, 1997 by Thunder's Mouth Press. Appears by
permission of the publisher, Thunder's Mouth Press.

Cover design by Amy Shoup
Text design by Michele Waters

ISBN 1-57224-338-4 Paperback

Printed in the United States of America

New Harbinger Publications' Web site address: www.newharbinger.com

05   04   03

10   9   8   7   6   5   4   3   2   1

First printing

This book is dedicated to all whose lives are driven or constricted by fear, anxiety, or panic. May you find peace, and may that peace penetrate the entire world.

Contents

part 1
getting oriented

part 2
practicing mindfulness

part 3
applying mindfulness to fear, anxiety, and panic

foreword

It gives me great pleasure to introduce this book to you. Jeff Brantley is a devoted practitioner of mindfulness meditation and a longtime teacher of mindfulness-based stress reduction (MBSR). Dr. Brantley has a great deal of clinical experience in working with people suffering from chronic stress, pain, and illness, and in particular, with chronic anxiety. This book is a welcome introduction to mindfulness practice for all those who experience anxiety in their lives. That turns out to be just about all of us at one time or another. For anxiety is rampant in our age, a kind of cosmic background radiation impinging continually on our individual and collective psyches and amassing a deep cumulative tension in the body. Currents of anxiety can be behind the smallest things we choose to do or refrain from trying, at work, at home, and in our interior lives. Knowingly and unknowingly, anxiety can shape the very fabric and direction of our lives, whether we have a diagnosed anxiety disorder or not.

For regardless of how well-off or healthy we may seem to be to others or even to ourselves, being human, we are hardly immune, at least on occasion, to the mental state we know as fear and to the short-

and long-term consequences it can have on the body and on how we carry ourselves and respond to stresses and challenges. For the most part, we tend to run from fear rather than to examine it. It remains unexamined precisely because it is so terrifying a prospect actually to take a peek at it, and to acknowledge to ourselves how fear-based our lives and our decisions can be, and how inexperienced we are at facing and freeing ourselves from the inner workings of such pervasive and potentially destructive mental states.

But taking a peek and letting yourself actually feel the fear in your body is worth doing, strange as that may at first seem. Anxiety, it turns out, can be a great teacher. And the lessons to be learned if we can be mindful, calm, and clear-sighted in the face of fear, anxiety, and perpetual worrying are profound. The mind's anxious preoccupations, proliferations, vexations, and frustrations sometimes seem endless. But, as Dr. Brantley points out, they do not have to be ultimately confining or imprisoning. And over time, their "volume" in our lives can turn itself down considerably.

This book and the methods it presents can serve as a remarkable pathway to freedom from the imprisonment of chronic anxiety and panic, at whatever level they may manifest in your life. Mindfulness practice can serve as a doorway giving ready access to deep and profoundly healthy dimensions of your being that you may have been ignoring for too long, to what you might call your "best self." It turns out you do not have to fix anything, or make anything go away to get in touch with yourself in this way. As you will learn in this book, all that is asked of you is that you start paying attention to aspects of your life and your immediate experience that you may have previously pretty much taken for granted. Several medical studies that we conducted on people with anxiety and panic disorder referred to our clinic for training in MBSR showed that the participants benefited enormously from this systematic cultivation of attention, as described in this book with great thoroughness and clarity by Dr. Brantley.

From the point of view of MBSR, no matter what has transpired in your life up to this point, no matter what you are facing, no matter what feels "wrong," you are fundamentally okay, worthy, and secure in this very moment, even if you don't know it or feel it. This is so even when the outer world appears overwhelmingly disorienting and threatening, even when the interior world of your own mind feels tumultuous and shaky. But of course, you have to test out for yourself whether this is indeed true. The great adventure of mindfulness is to discover or recover that intrinsic, spacious, secure, aware, innermost quality of your being, way deeper than your thoughts and feelings, and allow it to inform and guide the moment-to-moment conduct of your life, even, if not especially, when faced by great inner or outer turmoil.

This approach involves intentionally cultivating greater intimacy with the interior landscape of your life—that is with your mind and your body and the breath that serves as a convenient link between them in the only moment you ever have, namely this one. That is what mindfulness offers you. It is not a matter of eradicating anxiety but rather becoming intimate with it through awareness because it is already here. In making room for it, you discover that the anxiety you are experiencing in any moment is not you, but merely a constellation of strongly habitual thoughts, feelings, and body sensations that you may be investing with a power they would not otherwise have over your life, and which might therefore severely restrict your options for responding effectively in situations you find stressful and which trigger these habitual patterns of reactivity. You discover "you" are mysteriously larger than these conditioned patterns hijacking the mind and body, and that your awareness of anxiety, fear, and worry is not anxious at all. It is already okay. Learning to "inhabit" your own awareness and deepen its scope and stability is a way give you back to yourself and add significant degrees of freedom to your life.

The great painter, Georgia O'Keefe, once said: "I've been absolutely terrified every moment of my life, and I've never let it keep me from doing a single thing that I want to do." If we are willing to patiently and lovingly watch our own minds, our own mental turmoil, our own fears and hesitations and despairing thoughts, and our own body reactions to those very thoughts, we will come to see how much bigger we are than they are. We will discover something of our own truest nature.

It may come as a surprise to experience for yourself how large and beautiful and transparent you already are. This book is an invitation to practice mindfulness, whether on any given day you feel like it or not, as if your life depended on it . . . and be surprised.

—Jon Kabat-Zinn, Ph.D.
Professor of Medicine *emeritus*
University of Massachusetts Medical School
Center for Mindfulness in Medicine, Health
Care, and Society

acknowledgments

In writing this book, I am once again in awe of the amazing inter-connectedness of life. I would like to thank and to acknowledge the following people. Without them, this book would not have been possible.

My parents, Garland and Irene Brantley, for giving me this life, and their love and support.

My mother-in-law, Mary Principe, whose love and generosity has made so many things possible.

My sister Carolyn, and all my kin, by blood and by marriage, who have been there for me over the years.

All the friends and colleagues whose support and examples have inspired and strengthened me.

My patients and their families, whose burdens and courage have taught and enriched me.

My spiritual guides and meditation teachers, among them especially the following.

Roger Walsh, MD, who showed me how mindfulness could exist in academic medicine and as part of medical education.

Joan Halifax, Ph.D., who has been a dear friend and guide over the years, always pointing to the next horizon.

The monks and nuns of the Amaravati Buddhist Monastery, especially Ajahn Sucitto and Ajahn Sundara, for their example and inspired teachings.

The teachers and staff of the Insight Meditation Society in Barre, Massachusetts, for providing a place—visible and invisible—that supports awakening.

To all the wonderful people working in integrative medicine at Duke and elsewhere who value mindfulness and its place in the healing process.

To Marty Sullivan, MD, whose vision, courage, and efforts made Mindfulness-Based Stress Reduction at Duke possible.

To my fellow instructors in the Mindfulness-Based Stress Reduction Program and our staff: thanks for all you do. Because of you, our program, and my own practice, is immeasurably enriched.

To everyone at New Harbinger, and espeically, my editors Jueli Gastwirth and Jess Beebe: thanks for all your wisdom and skill in making this book happen.

A special acknowledgment to Jon Kabat-Zinn: thank you for the leadership in bringing mindfulness forward all these years, and especially for the friendship and support you have given me.

And finally, a very special acknowledgment to my wife, Mary Mathews-Brantley. Without your love, wisdom, and support, this book would definitely not have happened. Many thanks!

introduction

If you are reading this book, you are probably feeling some kind of disturbance in your life. It may take the form of fear, anxiety, or even panic and dread. It could be about something known or unknown, something that has happened or that may happen. It could be about you or about someone close to you.

If you are feeling worry or upset, fear or anxiety, you are probably looking for a way to find peace and simplicity in your life. You may be searching for a place to stand in order to face the fullness and intensity of life.

Fear, Worry, Upset, and Anxiety Are Common Today

Uncertainty seems to grow daily in life all around us. Newspaper headlines scream of terrorist threats, international conflict, environmental disasters, dishonesty and corruption in government and business. Catholic priests are accused of sexual abuse. Schoolchildren are searched for weapons because some of their fellows have chosen to become mass murderers.

Life grows busier for people everywhere. Information streams at us from all directions and knows no boundary. Cell phones, pagers, voice mail, e-mail, laptop computers, and the Internet contribute to the never ending workday as people can be reached anytime, anywhere, for any reason. More and more people expect to be—or are asked to be—always available.

Unfortunately, these are not the only sources of fear, worry, and anxiety in life today. It remains for each of us to add our own unique and personal items to the list of national and global concerns.

Whether it is trouble at work, worry over finances, or concern for the well-being of our children, the health of our parents, the illness of a friend, the condition of our neighborhoods or schools, or even our own health, it can appear that there is no end to the flood of problems and stressors we face. Personal life can feel more and more out of control and out of balance.

A kind of low-grade panic becomes the standard operating mode. With it comes increasing discomfort, ill ease, and the loss of joy in living.

The idea of burnout takes on a deeper and more personal meaning. People seek relief in food, drugs, sex, movies, television, and even more work! Yet the ill ease remains. Too often, the things we use for relief create more problems. We long for a simpler life. In the world's wealthiest country, we may have discovered, in the words of the meditation teacher Christina Feldman (2001, p. ix), "having is not the same as happiness."

The health consequences of this discomfort and ill ease grow clearer as well. We seek and receive treatment for many and varied stress-related illnesses. Sales of prescription medications to treat depression and anxiety are enormous. Americans spend billions of dollars annually on complementary and alternative treatments in addition to mainstream Western medicine.

When Worlds Meet and Merge

We live in truly interesting times. In the pages of this book, you will find ideas and information from two apparently very different worlds.

From the world of evidence-based Western medicine, you will hear about the connection between mind and body, and about the vital role of thoughts and emotions in health and illness. In addition, you will learn more about the body's fear system and how it functions and malfunctions to produce anxiety and panic.

From the world of meditation and inquiry into meaning and purpose, you will learn about the practice of mindfulness and the potential for presence and stillness in every human being. You will discover that you have the same potential for awareness and peace as everyone else, and that you have an untrained mind with its own hindrances, just like everyone else.

In a curious sense, this book represents a major trend in modern society: we now see the crossover between traditions and areas of knowledge and information previously regarded as quite separate and distinct. In this book, you will find references to current medical views alongside citations from meditation teachers of international renown.

This convergence of worlds opens many questions. At present there are not so many answers. But the fact is that treatments offered by Western medical science do not work for everyone. This is especially true of treatments for anxiety and panic.

Consequently, many health-care providers have been looking to other sources for ways to promote healing and health. This has led many to investigate the health and healing potential of meditation. As a result, meditation has become much more widely used in Western health-care settings over the past twenty-five years.

Who This Book Is Written For

This book is designed to help anyone who is burdened by fear, worry, anxiety, or panic and would like to do something to improve the situation.

If you have been diagnosed with an anxiety disorder and are being treated for that, or if you have no diagnosis but feel the pain of fear, worry, anxiety, or panic from whatever source, the approach in this book is directed at you.

Health-care providers who seek to aid those beset by fear, worry, anxiety, or panic will find useful information about mindfulness and meditation, as well as valuable support for their own meditation practice experience.

The Invitation, Challenge, and Opportunity of Mindfulness

The approach offered in this book relies on a basic human quality called *mindfulness*. Mindfulness may be understood as friendly, nonjudging, present-moment awareness. To succeed with this approach, you must learn and use a variety of meditation practices all directed at cultivating mindfulness.

As a training program in mindfulness aimed at dealing with fear, worry, anxiety, or panic, this book is an invitation, an opportunity, and a challenge as well.

It's an invitation in that the practices you will learn are a gentle call to stop and pay more attention to yourself and your life. They invite you to allow the awareness that flows naturally from that act of paying attention to inform how you live, each day and each moment, in each relationship, and with yourself. The invitation to practice mindfulness is an invitation to come into a new and more wholesome relationship with your experience—including fear, worry, anxiety, or panic.

As you practice mindfulness, you will have a rich opportunity to discover the inner space, stillness, and simplicity that are our natural heritage as human beings. It is a heritage we so often forget, yet we long for it deeply as our lives seem to spin more and more out of control. By taking this opportunity to learn and develop skills for being more present, you can realize in yourself the spaciousness and stillness that can safely contain even the most anxious moments of heart and mind.

But be warned! Doing what is asked here is a challenge. Mindfulness is not always easy to achieve or to sustain. You will have moments when you are filled with doubt and don't want to do any more meditation. There will be times when you don't like it. But you don't have to like it—just do it!

Cultivating awareness takes effort. Changing the habits of inattention and distraction we have developed over a lifetime is hard work. It is more hard work to allow yourself to stop and feel the present moment in its fullness. And it can be very hard work learning to open when you desire to close down, or learning to stay present for what is painful and unwanted in your life, especially when it is clouded by fear and great anxiety.

Kindness and Compassion

Mindfulness is practiced by paying attention on purpose, nonjudgmentally, and with a welcoming and allowing attitude. It means turning toward present-moment experience rather than away from it. Two qualities that support this way of relating to experience are kindness and compassion.

Kindness here means friendliness, or openheartedness. It enables you to welcome experience.

Compassion is usually associated with feelings of empathy and concern for pain or suffering in another. With this recognition of pain and suffering comes the wish for it to end. The practice of compassion carries with it a willingness to remain present and in contact with the painful situation, in the hope of bringing some measure of relief.

In this book, you will be invited to apply kindness and compassion to yourself and to the pain you feel from anxiety, fear, and panic. You will learn a specific meditation practice to cultivate these qualities in your life. For your mindfulness practice to deepen, it is very important that you open to and explore these qualities of kindness and compassion in yourself.

Mindfulness and compassion can free you from anxiety, fear, and panic as you learn to be present with an awareness that remains soft and open to pain and suffering. Learning to remain present with compassion for yourself as you bear the pain of anxiety, fear, and panic is an important part of your inner journey in meditation. As you learn through meditation to remain soft and openhearted in the presence of pain and fear, you will also learn what it means to be free of their control.

Self-Help Is Not a Substitute for Treatment

When you learn to do something to help yourself, you become an even more active and effective partner in your own treatment and health care. If you're receiving treatment for a diagnosed condition, this activity on your part can make a crucial difference in the progression and outcome of your illness. Self-help skills and practices can also have a significant and positive impact on your quality of life as you cope with the illness.

The mindfulness training offered in this book is intended to be a powerful self-help resource. However, it is in no way intended to be used as a substitute for any medical or psychological treatments you are already receiving.

While meditation is an extremely friendly and safe activity, please consult with your therapist or physician before doing the practices in this book if you are currently in treatment for any psychological or psychiatric condition. If you have a history of severe anxiety or trauma, you may need to use meditation in partnership with good treatment.

Mindfulness: A Way of Living, Not a Technique

Although many people learn to practice mindfulness as part of a larger treatment plan for a specific medical or psychological condition, it is a mistake to think of mindfulness as simply a treatment technique. While there is exciting evidence that practicing mindfulness might aid treatment, mindfulness itself is most powerful and most effective when practiced as a way of living.

Failure to appreciate this larger view of mindfulness ignores the ancient tradition of mindfulness as a practice pursued by countless people in many places and times. The essential power of the practice of mindfulness may be distorted or even lost by those who see it as only a technique.

Mindfulness is based in a daily meditation practice. In this book, you will be encouraged and guided in starting and maintaining your own meditation practice as a vehicle to cultivate mindfulness in your life. If you are interested in using mindfulness as part of a larger approach to treatment for an anxiety problem, the approach in this book will certainly help you. But you can enrich your life even more by considering mindfulness an integral approach to being in the world.

Experiential Learning

You must actually do the meditation practice to benefit. It will not help you much if all you do is read about mindfulness. In fact, some of it may sound crazy until you actually try it.

For example, in doing the body scan, you will be asked to breathe in and out of your toes. Sounds crazy, doesn't it? This instruction has to do with feeling the direct sensations of your breath and the sensations in your toes and holding all of that with steady attention. At this point, maybe that sounds crazy too.

Please make no judgments until you actually do the meditation practices. To realize what mindfulness means and how it can transform your life and your relationship to fear, anxiety, and panic, you must actually experience mindfulness through practice.

There is a capacity inside each of us to be calm and stable. We are capable of containing even the most intense fear and anxiety. This capacity is not something you can think about and understand. It is a direct experience that is always available. It is not a destination but a way of being.

Discovering your own capacity for calm, steadiness, and awareness requires turning inward and using your natural ability to pay attention. To turn inward this way *is* to meditate. This book is about learning to meditate in a very basic way that nourishes mindfulness, or friendly, nonjudging awareness.

The practices you will be invited to do in this book are about stopping and looking around. You will be invited to practice being and not doing. You will discover that it is possible to be more present with just about everything you do.

To support this, you will learn how to establish calm attention and a relaxed feeling in the body. A calm attention and a relaxed body are important elements of meditation. The practices in this book are compatible with any faith tradition or religious practice. They are simply about being present, in this calm and relaxed way, and opening to what is here—in us and in our life.

If you accept this challenge, commit to practicing meditation regularly, and have enough energy and discipline to make the practices in this book a part of your life, there is a very good chance you will begin a process of profound life change and transformation. Take as much time as you need to develop these practices. The important thing is that you remain committed.

In making this commitment to being aware and paying more careful attention, you will join people from all walks of life, cultures, and creeds who have discovered the profound richness that is available when we become mindful, or truly present to life. And you will realize what it truly means to calm your anxious mind.

The Goals of This Book

The goal of this book is to offer a self-guided training program in mindfulness meditation to ease the burden of fear, panic, and anxiety. It is suitable for people who wish to begin a mindfulness practice or to deepen a practice they already have. The meditation practices taught here are typical of those taught in a mindfulness-based stress-reduction program. They are accessible and easy to learn.

More specifically, as you read this book and learn the practices, you will gain

⁓ A direct and real sense of what it means to practice mindfulness. Armed with this understanding, you will be able to use mindfulness practice to more effectively manage fear, panic, and anxiety in your life.

⁓ A real and direct understanding of mindfulness as a way of living and being in life, with all the richness that brings.

Beyond managing fear, you will discover unexpected benefits of being more present for life.

⁓ A deep sense of your own wholeness and potential for healing and transformation through the process of facing fear, worry, and anxiety.

How to Use This Book

This book contains several different types of information. It provides current information and resources about mind-body health, mindfulness, meditation, and applications to conditions such as fear, worry, anxiety, and panic.

I include numerous examples of people facing situations of fear, anxiety, and panic. These examples come directly from my experience with hundreds of meditation students. Of course, their names and identifying personal details have been changed for confidentiality.

A large part of this book is devoted to the instruction and practice of mindfulness. Commentaries and guided meditation narratives focus on specific mindfulness practices. The power to heal and transform lies in doing the practices.

You will notice that there is great detail in the guided meditations. You might try breathing several times gently and naturally between each line of the narrative. This will help you do your practice better.

Reading can be distracting. It may work better to have someone read the guided meditation slowly to you. Alternatively, you could make your own tape or CD using your own voice or another person's voice reading the guided meditation phrases. Then practice by listening to your tape or CD.

The goal is to eventually learn to meditate without the guided meditation phrases. They are not the only words to use to do any of these mindfulness practices. The guided meditations give you a place to start. As you become more practiced and confident, you can let the guided phrases go. Learn to trust your own awareness and wisdom.

I will offer many suggestions about making these practices your own and weaving them into your life. Please make the commitment and find the discipline to do this. Move at your own pace. You might find you work with a particular practice quite some time before moving on. That is okay. When you have done them all, you will begin to see how they work together, but each works quite well by itself. Please give yourself—and each practice—a fair chance by working faithfully and patiently.

See for Yourself

You have to do the practices to get the benefit! It will not help you very much if all you do is read the book. Even if you go on to read a thousand other books about mindfulness, if you do not actually meditate, your reading will do you little good. The direct experience you gain through meditation is crucial. What you see for yourself makes all the difference.

In fact, if you have to make a choice between practicing mindfulness and reading about it, practice first. And keep practicing! If you practice, you will find that what you do read will make a lot more sense, and you will find that your practice will go deeper and farther.

Don't ever think you "know" what is happening. Words, thoughts, and the illusion that we "know" are very tricky! It is better to practice not knowing. Don't think your ideas are the way it really is. The map is not the territory.

And when you do the practices and you start to feel some benefit, don't stop. Keep practicing! Don't try to make something come back or happen again. Just keep paying attention. You already have what you need to succeed. You are starting a journey down a path of awakening. On that journey, you are required to do some work, be persistent, and keep coming back to it even when you feel lost or discouraged.

If you stay on this path of awakening, your life will change in unexpected and wonderful ways. It is guaranteed!

part 1

getting oriented

chapter 1

a mindful approach to fear and anxiety

From the point of view of mindfulness, everything happens in the present moment. All we have is the present moment. What we call the past is a memory that actually occurs in the present moment, and what we call the future is something we are imagining or planning now—in the present moment. This present-moment focus is crucial to understanding all our experiences, including fear, anxiety, and panic. In the present moment, the mind and body interact with the environment in an ever changing and dynamic way.

If you desire to teach yourself a better way to manage fear, anxiety, and panic, then the lesson must begin with what is happening in the present moment. Through meditation, you learn to establish and maintain attention in the present moment. From this base of attention, awareness or mindfulness produces clarity and understanding. From understanding flows constructive and compassionate action.

Physical experience is deeply interconnected with psychological and emotional experience moment by moment. Physical sensations can trigger thoughts (as when you perceive pain in your knee as arthritis and begin to think of the story of your arthritis and your fear of arthritis), and thoughts can stimulate physical responses (as when you recall an angry outburst in a meeting, and your neck and shoulders immediately tense up).

Fear, anxiety, and panic also occur as experience, flowing into and out of the present moment. They command physical, psychological, and emotional attention as well. To view them as experience in the present moment may seem radical. You have probably thought of fear, anxiety, or panic more as problems you had to deal with, or as conditions (or even illnesses) that too often seemed to have the upper hand in your life.

You may even have come to identify with them. Have you referred to yourself as "an anxious person" or "a frightened person," in a way that suggests that anxiety or fear is mostly who you are, or mostly what your life is about?

In fact, such a limiting definition of who you are is completely inaccurate, even if:

⌒ at times anxiety is so strong you fear you are going crazy

⌒ it seems that your heart is always pounding

⌒ you avoid people and places because you are afraid you will make a fool of yourself

⁓ you are a perfectionist tormented by guilt because you feel like you never measure up

The truth is that you are much more than any momentary experience, even if that experience is an intense one like fear, anxiety, or panic.

You have the capacity to recognize this and to reconnect with the whole of who you are. By teaching yourself the art of attention and awareness, or mindfulness, you will understand deeply what it means to be present, and how you can be free from the limitations and distortions of fear, anxiety, and panic.

Understanding Fear, Panic, and Anxiety

Both fear and anxiety share the intensely unpleasant feelings of dread and foreboding, but when the source of the dread is a threat that can be identified, the feeling is called *fear*. Fear may be defined as the feeling of agitation, apprehension, dread, or even terror caused by the presence or nearness of a danger or threat.

For example, you see a snake and feel fear. Or you find a lump in your breast and feel fear. Or you hear on your car radio that a tornado has been sighted in your area of town, and you feel fear. Or as you get near the top of a high cliff, you slip and fall toward the edge, and you feel fear.

When the feelings of dread and foreboding are not so clearly associated with an identified danger or threat, they are called *anxiety*. Indeed, this difficulty or inability to identify exactly what you are anxious about is a hallmark of anxiety.

The word "anxiety" comes from the Latin word *anxius*, which means a condition of agitation and distress. With anxiety, this agitation and distress is felt deeply—in the mind and body—in the present moment. The fearful feeling is more internal and seems to be in response to something threatening but hazy, something vague or far away. You cannot identify the danger but feel the fear anyway.

For example, you have awakened every morning for weeks feeling afraid, and you do not know why. Or you know it is "irrational," but you are terrified to ride the elevator in the building where you work.

Or you are so frightened about flying that you have turned down job opportunities that would have required air travel.

Worry is the mind's expression of anxiety. It can be understood as the combination of the physical experience of anxiety (fear without the identified danger) and the thoughts, stories, images, and other cognitive activity driven by the anxiety.

For example, you cannot plan a vacation without thinking about all the things that could go wrong. Or you cannot stop anticipating every detail of a meeting with your boss scheduled in two weeks. Or you cannot stop worrying about how dangerous the wiring is in your home since a neighbor's house caught fire.

When the feeling of fear is intense, sudden, and overwhelming but comes without any apparent cause, it is called *panic*. Panic attacks can come from out of the blue, with no apparent cause. People experiencing such acute apprehension and intense fear often think they are about to die. Panic is so unpleasant that people usually begin to modify and restrict their activities because of it.

It is important to acknowledge that whether it is fear or anxiety, whether the danger is present or vague, the experience of the *fear reaction*—what you feel as fear or anxiety—in the present moment is compelling.

The fear reaction is expressed and experienced in the body, in the mind, and in behavior. When you experience the fear reaction, you endure some (or even many) of the following as the physical, cognitive, emotional, and behavioral elements flow into and out of the present moment.

Physical Experience

Your heart pounds and races. Your muscles tense and tighten. You sweat, tremble, or shake. You feel tingling sensations or numbness. You may have a sense of choking or difficulty breathing. You may have discomfort or even pain in your chest. A feeling of queasiness, abdominal distress, or nausea often arises. Headaches and backaches are common. You may feel dizzy, unsteady, or like you are about to faint.

Psychological and Emotional Experience

The interior psychological and emotional experience is also intense. You may have feelings of unreality and dissociation. You fear losing control or going crazy. If the anxiety is very intense, you may wonder if you are about to die. Your ability to concentrate and to think clearly is disturbed. Your mind is confused. Thoughts repeat. You may become preoccupied with a particular thought or idea, so that you feel "stuck" on a theme.

Feelings of despair and hopelessness arise. You feel helpless or powerless to do anything about these deeply unpleasant feelings and the burden they create.

Behavioral Experience

Anxiety may manifest itself in your behavior. For example, you may avoid people or situations. You may develop elaborate rituals that must be performed before you can do any other activities. Or you may be bound by repetitive compulsions such as hand washing or door checking that interfere with the flow of daily life.

When the fear reaction arises repeatedly and persists over time, it is called *chronic*. We could say that to call fear or anxiety chronic means that it is a frequent visitor to the present moment. Chronic fear and anxiety can affect your relationships, work, social life, personal health, and inner life.

When you suffer from chronic fear and anxiety, your feelings of restlessness and ill ease grow stronger. Your energy is low, and you are easily fatigued. Sleep is disturbed. You may be unable to think or concentrate. You may feel like your mind is going blank. Participation in conversations, even social ones, can become difficult. You may feel more irritable, lash out at others, become overly critical, or withdraw from people. The use of alcohol and drugs (prescribed or recreational) often increases.

Normal or Excessive Anxiety?

Everyone experiences anxiety. The arousal from anxiety, in its milder forms, can actually be helpful. Anxiety increases your attention, as when a barely avoided collision brings your attention back to your car and the traffic for the rest of your drive home. Mild anxiety can enhance performance and productivity, as when speakers become more focused or athletes are motivated to put aside all other distractions immediately before the game begins.

Everyone worries. Many people regard some worry as good. In its milder forms, worry can warn of danger or point toward useful action.

When anxiety is moderate or high rather than mild, however, the results are usually not so positive. The experience of moderate levels of anxiety can be notably uncomfortable. This level of anxiety can lead to cognitive disorganization and to some or many of the physical symptoms mentioned earlier. High levels of anxiety definitely interfere with daily life and function, and, if chronic, may need professional treatment.

You may have mild, moderate, or even occasional high levels of anxiety and *not* have an anxiety disorder. Just reacting to life can evoke those feelings.

The following criteria can help you understand the difference between normal and excessive anxiety. It is the presence of excessive or *pathologic* anxiety that defines *anxiety disorders*. Excessive anxiety

~ Has very little recognizable cause and is present for no good reason.

~ Has a disturbing level of intensity well beyond everyday anxiety.

~ Lasts longer than everyday anxiety, up to weeks or months at times.

~ Has a significant and detrimental impact on living. In fact, the pain may lead to destructive behaviors such as withdrawal, avoidance, or abuse of food, alcohol, or other substances.

Anxiety disorders are the most prevalent of all psychiatric conditions. They are a huge burden for the afflicted individuals and their loved ones, and also for society through lost work productivity and the high utilization of health-care resources by those suffering from anxiety disorders. Anxiety disorders afflict 15.7 million people in the United States each year, and 30 million people in the United States at some point in their lives (Lepine 2002).

The American Psychiatric Association (1994) recognizes ten distinct anxiety disorders, plus "anxiety disorder not otherwise specified." From the viewpoint of mindfulness, the important thing to remember is that the characteristic symptoms in these disorders—combinations of physical arousal, intrusive and disturbing thoughts, and intensely unpleasant sensations—all occur in the present moment. Excessive anxiety is the fear response happening in the present moment for no apparent reason, or for a reason that does not justify intensity of the fear.

Self-help is a vital component of a comprehensive treatment plan, but it is not a substitute for needed treatment. If you think you may have a diagnosable anxiety disorder, you should consider consulting a qualified mental health professional.

Causes of Anxiety and Anxiety Disorders

Our understanding of the causes of anxiety and pathologic anxiety has increased dramatically in recent years as the physical and neurochemical pathways of fear and anxiety have been studied. However, much more research is needed, and our understanding is far from complete at present. This incomplete understanding is reflected in the variety of models that seek to explain anxiety and its pathologic forms.

Current understanding of fear and anxiety identifies the causes as a powerful interaction of biology, cognitive-emotional influences, and stress.

Biology

Each person has a body. Your body is the fundamental biological and neurological platform from which your moment-by-moment experience and interaction with life occurs. Crucial elements of the body's role in anxiety lie in the function of the central and peripheral nervous systems, and in the array of organs and systems that respond to and communicate with the nervous system.

Since the body is vital to experience, it makes sense that the genetic influence on anxiety would be important. Although there is limited evidence at present, it does appear that, to some degree, anxiety disorders are inherited. This inheritance is probably mediated through differences in each person's sensitivity in key areas of the brain. These areas vary in their response to the array of stress modulators and neurotransmitters active in the brain and body. However, there is much more to be learned about how this tendency to be anxious is passed on from generation to generation and how this tendency should be handled in treatment.

In some ways, you have little control over what your body does reactively, but your body is intelligent and can be trained. There is growing evidence that people can learn to exert considerable influence over the reactions and ongoing activities of the body by learning and using a variety of *mind-body* methods. The meditation and relaxation practices you will learn in this book are potent examples of the mind-body connection.

Certain medical conditions, medicines, and other substances can contribute to or cause anxiety and panic attacks. A detailed discussion of these is beyond the scope of this book. However, if anxiety interferes significantly in your life, please consult a medical professional to determine if there is a treatable medical cause for the anxiety. Consider your own use of medications and other substances, since the list of anxiety-causing agents is quite long and includes such common items as caffeine, tobacco, and aspirin.

Cognitive-Emotional Influences

A second important contributing factor in anxiety and panic seems to be the effect of childhood experiences and the family environment on a person's self-perception, ways of relating to others, and ways of handling the demands and stressors of living.

For example, factors such as your view of the world as threatening or supportive, your level of self-confidence and belief in your ability to handle stressors, and how you handle and express feelings (toward yourself and toward others) have all been shown to have a major impact on health and the ability to cope. Each of these sets of views arises repeatedly in you—in the present moment—and in turn influences how you experience what is happening and what you do about it.

Your experience of fear and anxiety is directly affected by the thoughts, perceptions, and emotions you have in that moment. Just as you can learn skills to work with the physical reactions of fear and anxiety in the present moment, you can also work with these powerful attitudes and views. It is crucial to realize that views and patterns of reactivity can be recognized, they can be changed, and they can be replaced with more adaptive and healthy views and patterns.

Stress

The third major factor contributing to the development of anxiety—and especially anxiety disorders—is the cumulative or long-term role of stress. There can be many sources of this chronic stress, but the effects of leaving it unmanaged are clear. Chronic stress greatly increases the likelihood of illness and the breakdown of physical, emotional, social, and even spiritual life.

Treating Anxiety Disorders

The most widely used mainstream approaches to treating anxiety are medications, specific types of psychotherapy, or both.

Commonly prescribed medications include *tricyclic antidepressants* and another class of antidepressants known as *selective serotonin reuptake inhibitors*. In some cases, *monoamine oxidase inhibitors* may be prescribed instead.

The most common psychotherapies are *behavioral therapy* and *cognitive behavioral therapy*. Behavioral therapy uses methods such as relaxation training and gradual exposure to whatever frightens a person as a means to cope with fears. Cognitive behavioral therapy teaches people to recognize thought patterns, body sensations, and situations that trigger fears, and to react differently.

However, even after a number of years of research and concerted efforts to develop more effective treatment for anxiety disorders, the currently available treatments do not work for everyone with an anxiety disorder.

Because of this, health-care providers and researchers continue to seek new approaches. In recent years, self-help methods, including meditation, have gained attention. There is a growing recognition that each person has an important part to play in their own treatment and recovery.

Meditation methods that specifically emphasize mindfulness are being used more often in clinical treatment settings. Medical literature concerned with anxiety treatments is beginning to reflect this trend. The term *mindfulness-based cognitive therapy* is gaining popularity, and a growing number of professionals are working to research and apply this combination of mindfulness, meditation, and cognitive behavioral therapy.

John Teasdale, Zindel Segal, and colleagues (2000) have published research that suggests a mindfulness-based cognitive therapy approach can prevent relapse and recurrence in major depression. In 2002 Lizabeth Roemer published a comprehensive review of cognitive approaches to anxiety and discussed the role of mindfulness in treating anxiety. She concluded that mindfulness may be particularly useful for individuals with generalized anxiety disorder. Although both articles caution against drawing premature conclusions, the authors make a strong case for exploring this interface of mindfulness and therapeutic approaches.

Keep in Mind

Fear, anxiety, and panic can be overwhelming experiences. They can also be understood as experiences that flow into and out of the present moment. This is true of either normal or excessive anxiety.

You can learn to handle fear and anxiety by bringing relaxation and attention into your life and keeping a present-moment focus. Because fear and anxiety happen in the present moment, it is vital that you learn to establish yourself—and remain—in the present moment in order to manage them. Mindfulness meditation practice establishes attention in the present moment. There is a growing body of evidence that developing a daily practice of meditation which emphasizes mindfulness (friendly, nonjudging awareness) is something you can do to help yourself manage fear, anxiety, and panic.

chapter 2

paying attention on purpose

P racticing mindfulness means learning to relax and stay present with a nonjudging and friendly awareness. Mindfulness is cultivated by paying attention—on purpose and carefully—to the contents of this moment in a friendly and allowing way. As we are using the term in this book, mindfulness is developed through a daily practice of meditation.

To teach yourself a better way to manage fear, anxiety, and panic, it is important for you to learn to relax, and practice this way of "paying attention on purpose." As you develop your capacity to be mindful through meditation, you will discover that you can be relaxed *and* aware. You will begin to relate *to* the experiences of fear, anxiety, or panic rather than *from* them or as if they are who you are.

As you increasingly come to see these experiences as conditions in the present moment instead of as your enemy or your "problem," they will no longer dominate your life. You will make more effective responses to them.

In this book, several themes will appear and reappear.

⌒ Although you may be struggling with fear, anxiety, or panic, *you already have what you need to transform your life.* Mindfulness, kindness, and compassion are within you.

⌒ *The ground for this transformation is mindful presence,* which is nonjudging, nonstriving, accepting, present-moment awareness. The emphasis when practicing mindfulness is on being, not doing.

⌒ *Your experience of fear, anxiety, or panic is transformed when you make it the direct object of mindfulness.* In a mindfulness-based approach, the instruction is to turn toward fear, anxiety, or panic when they arise. You do not recoil, run away, or try to suppress them.

⌒ *This approach to fear, anxiety, and panic works best when you make mindfulness a way of living.* To approach life mindfully is to meet and connect with each experience as it arises and flows through the present moment of life. Mindfulness will not work so well if you think of it as a method or technique and wait to use it only when fear, anxiety, or panic is here and troubling you. Mindfulness becomes a way of living when you ground it in a daily practice of meditation and extend this practice into your life.

~ Specific meditation practices, including those in this book, are meant to assist you in making mindfulness a way of living. *The focus varies in different practices, yet all aim to help you be present for the moments of your life,* regardless of what is happening in and around you during those moments.

Does Practicing Mindfulness Really Help?

The only way to know whether mindfulness will work for you is to try it. However, a growing, encouraging body of medical research suggests that people facing a wide variety of problems, including anxiety and panic, can enjoy significant benefits when they develop mindfulness through a committed practice of daily meditation.

Mindfulness itself is a basic human quality. It is the capacity for conscious presence. It is the awareness that is friendly, nonjudging, and allowing.

People have systematically cultivated this quality through meditation for thousands of years. Historically, the goal has been to enhance spiritual practice and to aid the realization of a higher purpose and meaning in life.

Since the 1960s, when a large-scale social transformation sparked interest among Westerners in meditation, Eastern spirituality, and altered states of consciousness, there has been growing interest in meditation and mindfulness as it relates to health and healing.

Lyn Freeman (Freeman and Lawlis 2001) points out in *Mosby's Complementary and Alternative Medicine* that despite thousands of years of human experience with meditation, "it has only been in the last twenty-five years that meditation has been researched as a medical intervention in Western cultures. (p. 168)" According to Freeman and Lawlis, this research has focused on four separate forms of meditation: *transcendental meditation; respiratory one method,* developed by Herbert Benson; *clinically standardized meditation,* developed by Carrington and others; and *mindfulness meditation.*

Freeman notes that mindfulness meditation "differs significantly from the other three" in that the first three are all essentially *concentrative* techniques that instruct the meditator to focus attention on a single object, such as a phrase or a sound. Mindfulness is a *nonconcentrative* technique in which the person widens his or her consciousness "to include the observation, in a nonjudgmental way, of his or her mental activities and thoughts" (Freeman and Lawlis 2001, p. 168).

Jon Kabat-Zinn pioneered the medical use of mindfulness meditation when he founded the Stress Reduction Clinic at the University of Massachusetts Medical Center in 1979. The approach used in that program has come to be known as *mindfulness-based stress reduction* (MBSR). In MBSR, Kabat-Zinn and his colleagues used a combination of mindfulness meditation methods and mindful yoga to help thousands of participants cope more effectively with stress, pain, and illness.

Mindfulness and Medical Research

Since 1979, a number of clinical studies have documented the health benefits of practicing mindfulness. Mindfulness has been reported to be associated with improvements in levels of anxiety, panic, and general mood disturbance. In addition, mindfulness has been reported to be useful as a self-regulation practice in a variety of other conditions.

Kabat-Zinn and colleagues (1992) published results from the Stress Reduction Clinic documenting significant reductions in symptoms of anxiety and panic in patients with generalized anxiety disorder, panic disorder, and panic disorder with *agoraphobia* (fear of being in a place or situation from which escape is difficult).

In 1995, J. Miller and colleagues published results of a follow-up report on the earlier group studied by Kabat-Zinn in 1992. They found that after three years, a majority of subjects still practiced meditation and had maintained significant improvements in reduced anxiety.

Speca and colleagues (2000) reported significant benefits from mindfulness meditation in a group of cancer patients. Meditation reduced mood disturbance in general and significantly reduced depression, anxiety, anger, and confusion.

In 1998, Shapiro and Schwartz reported findings from a group of medical and premedical students who practiced mindfulness-based stress reduction. They found significant reductions in overall psycho-logical distress, including anxiety and depression. They also reported increased levels of empathy and increased scores on a measure of spiri-tual experiences.

John Teasdale, Zindel Segal, and colleagues (2000) reported results from a multicenter trial in Canada and the United Kingdom. They studied the application of mindfulness with cognitive therapy to prevent relapse in people with major depressive illness. For people with three or more previous episodes of major depression, they found that mindfulness practices combined with cognitive therapy principles significantly reduced the risk of relapse.

Linehan (1993a, 1993b) described the use of mindfulness tech-niques as a way of integrating acceptance into change-based psychotherapies. Her work has focused on individuals diagnosed with borderline personality disorder, and the model she developed, *dialecti-cal behavior therapy* (DBT), has been widely replicated.

Other reports support the use of mindfulness meditation in chronic pain (Kabat-Zinn et al. 1986), fibromyalgia (Kaplan, Goldenberg, and Galvin-Nadeau 1993), psoriasis (Kabat-Zinn et al. 1998), with a popula-tion of inner-city residents (Roth 1997), in binge eating (Kristeller and Hallett 1999), and stress reduction (Astin 1997).

There is still much to be understood about how practicing mind-fulness actually helps in these various conditions. That it helps seems clear.

Keep in Mind

In this book we will look at some of the basic understanding about fear systems and anxiety, and the role of thoughts and attitudes in health. Medical science has not yet reached a final conclusion about how anxiety and panic happen or how they should best be treated.

By learning to be present and to stay connected with your body and mind and what is happening in the present moment, you have your best chance of understanding your own experience of fear, anxi-ety, and panic. Out of that understanding, you will make the most effective response for healing.

There is a promising new body of research that supports mindful-ness meditation as an aid in a variety of medical conditions, including anxiety and panic.

chapter 3

the body and its fear system

Y ou already know how it feels to be afraid. It has been said that
fear is one of the most basic of all human emotions. A key point
here is that fear is something you can actually *feel*. The racing
heart, the tensing muscles, the heightened sense of alertness, and
the sweaty palms can all be felt. Deeper in the body, in the layers of
muscle and in the visceral organs, you can feel sensations, movements, gripping, and hardening.

You may have noticed that the feelings in your body associated
with fear are very similar to feelings you may have associated with anxiety, worry, or panic. Based on what we know about the mind-body
connection, this is not surprising.

In the 1990s, research related to the brain's anatomy, neuro-
chemistry, and electromagnetic operation was intense and productive.
We now know much more about how the brain functions in both normal and abnormal conditions. These discoveries are quite relevant as
you practice mindfulness and face fear and anxiety in your own life.

Research is beginning to reveal how deeply the body and mind
are interconnected. The emerging picture is both complex and fasci-
nating. As a human being, you are in a dynamic, continuously changing, and interactive relationship involving your mind and body and the
surrounding environment.

This relationship requires that you have functioning systems to
take in information via the senses. More systems must then act to
assess, compare, and process the new information. Finally, you need
systems to store, manage, and retrieve the information for future use.

Your brain and nervous system communicate with each other and
the rest of your body constantly to assess and maintain contact with
your surrounding external environment; to generate, measure, and
direct your responses to that environment; and to maintain the
moment-by-moment conditions of your interior environment.

As a key part in this interactive relationship, you have a built-in
emergency capacity called the *fight-or-flight reaction,* and you also
have a powerful built-in quieting and calming capacity called the *relaxation response.* Each of these responses is wired into us as human
beings. The responses function in such a way that they can happen in
your body yet outside of your conscious experience, but, importantly,
they can also be modified by your conscious experience.

Richard Davidson of the University of Wisconsin, Madison, is a
founder of the field of *affective neuroscience,* a branch of psychology
that studies the brain circuitry involved in the experience of emotions.

Dr. Davidson is quoted by Daniel Goleman in *Destructive Emotions* (2003): "One of the most exciting discoveries in neuroscience over the last five years is that the areas of the brain ... the frontal lobes, the amygdala, and the hippocampus, change in response to experience. They are the parts of the brain dramatically affected by the emotional environment in which we are raised and by repeated experience. (p. 189)" In other words, your brain function can actually change in response to experience. And what you do as part of that experience— for example, learning to meditate—has the power to change how your brain actually functions.

Fear is the reaction you feel in your body in the presence of an external threat or danger, and anxiety is the reaction you feel in your body when the danger or threat comes from within and is more vague. Either way, the fear system of the body is operating.

What exactly is happening in the brain and body when you experience the fight-or-flight response, or the fear reaction?

Fight or Flight

The fight-or-flight response is what you feel in your mind and body and call fear. This response is also sometimes called the *stress response*. Early researchers in the field of stress, such as Walter B. Cannon and Hans Selye, came to recognize and describe the arousal and physical changes animals experience in the face of danger or *stressors* (Freeman and Lawlis 2001). They saw that the increases in blood pressure, heart rate, muscle tone, and alertness—paired with the secretion of powerful hormones in the body—prepared the animal to defend itself or to flee. It was Cannon, working in the 1920s, who coined the term *fight-or-flight*. Selye, working in the 1950s, popularized the term *stress*.

It is interesting to note that Selye defined stress as a response to a stressor or demand. He viewed stress as the total response—mind and body—to whatever pressure or demand the animal (or person) faced.

To summarize, what we call fear, anxiety, or even panic is the felt or sensed component of a mind-body experience that is activated and controlled by a fear system wired into us as human beings.

The connections of the fear system involve several brain centers and body systems. The messages are transmitted over nerve pathways and through the blood as it circulates, and modulated by an astonishing array of stress hormones, proteins, and other neuroendocrine substances.

As a result, dramatic physical, cognitive, and emotional elements activate when the fear system alarms go off. This experience in its totality is designed to prepare you either to defend yourself or to flee from danger. When viewed as a response to a danger or stressor, this total mind-body response is also called *stress*.

When a person says "I feel stressed," what he or she actually feels is the various sensations of arousal and preparation to fight or flee that have arisen in the mind and body. The reason the feelings are so intense and unpleasant is usually that they have been building up over time as extended or chronic stress, or have developed especially strongly in a sudden, intense, and acutely stressful situation.

The dramatic physical changes are mediated by a variety of powerful chemical messengers (stress hormones) in the body. The best-known are *adrenaline* and *cortisol.*

Adrenaline plays a major role in the activation of the body for fight or flight. The racing heart, the rapid and shallow breathing, the profuse sweating, and the shaking and trembling are all due to the action of adrenaline.

The known effects of cortisol include mobilizing *glucose* (stored sugar) to provide immediate energy, increasing the body's sensitivity to other stress-related hormones, and inhibiting the immune and inflammatory responses.

In the *acute* or immediate stress response, adrenaline, cortisol, and all the other stress hormones are released and act on their target organs and tissues. As the threat subsides, the response eases, and the body returns to a more balanced state.

How the Fear System Operates

According to current research, the key to understanding the fear system lies in the *amygdala,* a small, almond-shaped structure located deep in the brain. This structure has powerful connections to a wide range of brain and body regions. It is the area of the brain most involved in fear.

Joseph LeDoux (1996) calls the amygdala the "hub in the wheel of fear. (p. 168)" To understand this, imagine the following.

In the center of a wheel is the amygdala. Surrounding it and connected to it by the spokes of the wheel are information-processing systems of the brain and body. These systems gather, send, and receive information constantly from the amygdala. This information includes

⌒ Direct sensory input (what is coming in from the eyes, ears, nose, tongue, and body).

⌒ Sensory input that has been processed by "higher centers" in the brain. For example, when the *sensory cortex* decides that the shape on the ground in front of you is a stick and not a snake, it sends signals to the amygdala to turn off the fear reaction.

⌒ Input not related to the senses, but associated with memories and contexts. For example, simply having a certain thought or memory may stimulate a feeling of fear or worry.

⌒ Input which can inhibit or turn down the amygdala's alarm. This inhibitory action is believed to be centered in an area at the front of the brain called the *prefrontal cortex.*

There is a very fast, direct pathway for input from any of the senses straight to the amygdala. The information is not "clean" or precise, but because it arrives so quickly, the body can respond almost immediately to danger.

A dog charges at you out of nowhere, a fire alarm goes off nearby, a truck runs the stop sign and almost hits you: such vivid sights and sounds can set off the amygdala. The message travels by this first, most direct route.

The amygdala sounds the alarm to the rest of the fear system. It activates the *hypothalamus* (a regulatory center in the brain), which fires signals to the *autonomic nervous system* (a part of the nervous system that acts without our conscious control), which in turn sends the signals to release the chemical messengers that act on organs and tissues to produce the fight-or-flight reaction.

There is a second, slower pathway that the incoming message also takes while the first, most immediate pathway is activating.

In the normal (nonstressed) order of brain function, various higher brain centers also process the incoming sensory data. They assess the information, compare it with similar information or experience stored in the memory, and interpret the situation as safe or dangerous. When the incoming information is judged safe, these centers have the power to override or inhibit the emergency alarm activated by the amygdala.

The fast pathway brings new sensory information to the amygdala and triggers the emergency response. The slower pathway processes the same information and can then communicate with the amygdala to either turn off or sustain the emergency response.

This means the higher centers must process the message correctly to turn off the emergency. The main function of the higher centers is to prevent the inappropriate emergency response from continuing.

If this inhibitory function of the higher centers—especially the prefrontal cortex—does not operate correctly, or if the higher centers mistakenly identify the input as dangerous, then the alarm sounds louder. Many researchers now believe that this dysfunction or failure of inhibition in the fear system contributes to the development of anxiety disorders. As Edmund J. Bourne (2000, p. 38) notes, "panic attacks are more likely to occur when this entire 'fear system' is overly sensitized, perhaps from having been previously activated too frequently, too intensely, or both." Bourne further suggests that "changes in this system can take place as a result of acute stress, or as the long-term result of multiple stresses over time."

The implications are clear. If anxiety arises out of fear system dysfunction, then management of anxiety depends on doing everything possible to enable the fear system to function properly. Developing skills in relaxation and present-moment awareness through meditation is an important way to support the healthy functioning of your body's fear system.

The Intelligent Body

Your body doesn't forget its experience with fear. It is quite intelligent. Your body has the ability to learn and to remember so that when a similar situation arises in the future, it can return automatically to the learned postures, movements, and responses.

This bodily intelligence is obvious when you think about such ordinary activities as walking, toothbrushing, or knitting. At some time (maybe years ago), you did not do the activity. Then you started it. At first it was not so smooth, but gradually your body learned how to move in that way, and it became "natural."

The body learns and remembers from every experience. For example, if you are in a traumatic or highly charged emotional situation and the fight-or-flight reaction is triggered, simply recalling the event at a later time is enough to arouse a similar physical experience in your body. Your body stores the memory of the situation, and remembering it activates the muscles into the particular patterns of tension they held and learned in the situation.

According to current understanding, memory is the result of several different systems at work in the brain and body. There are in fact different types of memory. *Emotional* or *fear* memory is stored and retrieved through a different system than is *conscious* or *declarative* memory. LeDoux states that "in the case of the amygdala system, retrieval results in expression of bodily responses that prepare for danger. . . . (p. 239)" When the body is aroused through its fear system, the arousal is remembered.

There is much yet to be learned about fear conditioning, body memory, and their relationship to anxiety. We do know that it is important to develop awareness of the body, to recognize thought and memory patterns, and to be patient in working with the deeply conditioned habits of the fear response, both physical and cognitive.

Anxiety and Chronic Stress

So the fear system is wired in, the brain may either override the emergency alarm triggered by the amygdala or sustain it, the override action depends upon processing activity in higher brain centers, the resulting fight-or-flight reaction is very intense and involves many body systems, and the body can remember its experience.

All of this was built into us as human beings in order to survive *immediate* danger. As a way of dealing with immediate danger, the fight-or-flight response makes sense and works pretty well. But what happens when the system developed to be a short-term answer to an occasional emergency becomes a long-term way of living?

Chronic stress is the persistent and repeated activation of the fear system over extended periods of time. In essence, the fight-or-flight response activates the body and readies it for vigorous physical action. But in the stressors that most of us encounter—the demands of daily life at work and in our family, for example—there is little relief or problem resolution from physical action. It literally doesn't help to fight or to run.

Medical research has shown some interesting and important effects of long-term arousal of the fear system. Shelley E. Taylor, a psychologist at the University of California at Los Angeles, has been a leader in understanding the effects of stress on health, and has done pioneering work in the different responses of men and women to stress. Taylor highlights the health effects of chronic stress in her 2002 book *The Tending Instinct*:

～～ Repeated fight-or-flight responses that increase heart rate and blood pressure contribute to the development of high blood pressure and heart disease.

～～ Repeated activation of stress hormones, especially the *glucocorticoids,* can lead to immune deficiencies, cause or worsen depression, and disrupt memory and other thought processes.

～～ If chronic stress leads to chronically elevated glucocorticoid levels, insulin activity can be impaired, and the risk for diabetes increases.

～～ The risk of cancer increases with chronic stress because the immune system—which normally catches cells in the earliest stages of cancerous growth—becomes less efficient.

Chronic stress can also be a major factor in the development of anxiety disorders. As Bourne (2000) states, if your weakest point "is the neuroendocrine and neurotransmitter systems of your brain, you will be more subject to developing a behavior disorder such as mood swings, generalized anxiety, or panic disorder. (p. 34)"

Chronic stress means chronic hyperarousal of the body through its fear system. The price for this is high, both physically and emotionally. Fortunately, there is good news. You have a balancing response to fight-or-flight wired into you. There are different ways to activate it, and meditation is one of them.

The Relaxation Response

The mind-body connection is at work again in the relaxation response, only this time it serves to reverse the activation characteristic of fight-or-flight. In short, heart rate slows. Breathing slows. Blood pressure comes down. Muscles soften and relax. There is a growing sense of ease and calm in the body and mind.

When the crisis or emergency has passed, the body restores balance through the action of the branch of the nervous system that controls calm, relaxation, and the resting body functions such as digestion and resting heart rate.

Herbert Benson, working at Harvard Medical School, is a pioneer in the field of mind-body medicine. In the late 1960s, he began studying subjects who practiced transcendental meditation. In this practice, the people meditating would sit quietly and repeat a phrase to themselves for a period of time. Whenever their attention wandered, they were instructed to resume repeating the phrase. Benson and colleagues measured physiological functions while the subjects were meditating and while they were engaged in everyday thoughts.

Benson (1993) summarized the remarkable results of this study: Breath rate, oxygen consumption, and levels of *blood lactate* (a chemical which in high levels has been associated with anxiety and in low levels with calm) all decreased markedly when the subjects were meditating. Also, brain waves associated with rest and relaxation (alpha, theta, and delta waves) increased in frequency, while beta waves (associated with normal waking activity) became fewer.

Benson had measured and named something meditation practitioners had known for thousands of years. Human beings have the ability, by directing attention and awareness, to enter extraordinary states of calm and relaxation.

Benson named this the *relaxation response,* and in the years since he coined that term, much has been learned about the body's ability to calm and relax, and the mind's power to activate this state.

In *Don't Panic,* R. Reid Wilson (1986) makes the point that many panic-prone people fear losing control if they relax or "let go." Wilson prefers the phrase *calming response* to relaxation response for this reason.

Whatever you choose to call it, the ability to calm and relax in the mind and body is an important ally. By learning to calm and ease your mind and body, you can begin to balance the distortions of hyperarousal from chronic stress. This will bring many benefits.

From the point of mindfulness, relaxation is not the ultimate goal. However, it is crucial to have a calm and relaxed attention in order to remain present and to be mindful. Learning to activate calm and ease in mind and body through concentrated attention will provide a strong foundation for the presence you will need to manage fear, anxiety, and panic.

Keep in Mind

The fear reaction is extremely powerful. It happens almost instantaneously. Yet each of us has the capacity to change how we react. Learning to meditate can give you the power you need to become more responsive and less reactive when fear happens.

chapter 4

anxiety and
the power
of the mind

In the early 1600s, at the height of the Renaissance, French philosopher René Descartes proclaimed, "I think, therefore I am." Living as he did in a time of intellectual awakening and the embrace of reason and knowledge, Descartes focused on the activity of thinking, especially questioning, and based identity there.

Today, in the early years of the twenty-first century, and from the perspective of mind-body medicine, it might be more accurate to say "I am what I think," or "I am not my thoughts," or even "I am more than my thoughts." These statements reflect more completely our emerging understanding of the connection of mind (the interior world of awareness that contains thoughts, feelings, memories, and more), through brain and body interrelationships and actions, to overall health.

What has long been observed in common language and folk wisdom about the power of the mind (and heart) to impact the body and health is now being documented by medical researchers. What you think and feel, how you talk to yourself, and what view you take about what is happening to you and around you has a powerful impact on your health and well-being.

The Power of Thought

Anxiety and panic often arise from fear-provoking thoughts or attitudes rather than from physical threats or danger. Indeed, the attitude or meaning in the mind is crucial to the perception of danger. In his 1986 book *Don't Panic,* R. Reid Wilson points out that "people, places, and events are panic-provoking only *after* we apply meaning to them. A store is just a store, a speech is just a speech, a drive is just a drive, until the brain interprets them as 'dangerous' or 'threatening.' To conquer panic, then, you must intervene at the *point of interpretation.* (p. 133)"

We know that the mind and the body are not separate. The links include the brain and the nervous system, the endocrine system, and the immune system. And, while there is still very little agreement or understanding about how crucial elements of mind such as consciousness actually happen in the brain and nervous system, much has been discovered about the connections and communications between brain and body.

Through its connections with the sense organs and the body, the brain receives information from the body and from the surrounding environment. The higher brain centers process this extraordinary mass of incoming information, store it as memory, and generate directions for the body and its various systems based on this processed information.

The body's fear system includes specialized areas of the brain that process sensory information and add contextual meaning to it before sending messages back to the body that modify the fight-or-flight reactions.

Other areas and systems of the brain provide familiar and crucial functions such as language, short- and long-term memory, attention, arousal, awareness, cognition, emotion, control of movement and activity, and social behavior.

The underlying physical and chemical base for this brain-body function is astounding. According to some estimates, there are as many as ten billion neurons in the human nervous system, wired together in enormously complex ways. It is this amazing array of information-systems activity that helps to create for each of us the sense of self and the moment-by-moment consciousness of body and the world outside the body.

So thoughts have power.

And they have the connections—through the brain-body links—to exert their power!

And what we call *self*, including our mind, is actually arising moment by moment (in ways that are not well understood by science) out of the interconnected activity of the brain and body interacting with the ever changing environment. The thoughts that occur, the emotions—such as fear and anxiety—that flavor each moment, and the deeper attitudes and views each person holds have an immediate and profound impact on the actual experience arising in each moment. This is because the thoughts, emotions, and views have direct and ongoing feedback into the systems *as they are processing* all the incoming and outgoing information.

From the standpoint of managing fear and anxiety, this is both good news and bad news.

The bad news is that fearful or anxious thoughts can continue to fuel and drive the body's fear system, mediated largely through connections with the amygdala. The input to the amygdala includes sensory and modified sensory data, plus data from other related nonsensory higher centers such as those involving thinking and memory.

All of this higher-level input is designed to enable an override of the amygdala's emergency messages to the rest of the body once the higher centers have had time to assess the situation. If the higher input (thinking) does not override the amygdala but rather stimulates it, then more fear-system activity happens. In other words, if the higher brain centers decide that the situation is dangerous, they confirm the amygdala's initial danger message rather than sending a reassuring message that everything is safe. This serves us well when the situation really *is* dangerous. But when our higher brain centers produce anxious thoughts about something threatening but vague—when we are in no real danger—our fear response stays turned on for no immediate reason.

The good news is that the higher centers *can* override the fear system and turn it down.

It is easy to see why becoming aware of your thoughts and learning to let them be instead of identifying with them might be very important in learning to manage fear and anxiety. Learning to recognize your thoughts and views, and to modify the ones that stimulate the fear system, is an incredibly powerful tool.

So, can you change how your brain functions? Can you alter the "hardwired" response by practicing meditation? There is growing evidence that the brain is much more malleable or *plastic* than was formerly believed. And the answer is yes, maybe you can change how your brain functions by meditating.

In a January 2003 article in the *Wall Street Journal*, columnist Sharon Begley reported on research by Richard Davidson soon to be published in the journal *Psychosomatic Medicine*. Dr. Davidson and his team studied brain function in employees of a local business. The employees were taught mindfulness meditation by Jon Kabat-Zinn over an eight-week period. Brain function in the employees was measured using MRI scans and EEG measurements before they learned to meditate, after eight weeks, and again sixteen weeks later.

The differences were clear. The results showed that activity in the frontal cortex in the meditators had shifted. There was an increased pattern of activity associated with feelings such as joy, happiness, and low levels of anxiety.

While this is only one study, it adds weight to the thesis that the links between the brain's thinking regions and feeling (emotional) regions is much more plastic than previously believed. This suggests that you can indeed learn to monitor moods and thoughts, learn to drop the disturbing ones, and enjoy less anxiety and more energy and joy as a result.

The Impact of Thoughts and Emotions on Health

Reflect on your own everyday experience for a moment. Have you noticed how holding a thought can lead to a body reaction? Are there particular stories or thought patterns that you have repeatedly? Have you recognized how they connect with feelings of fear, anxiety, or worry? Have you ever noticed how your own body is recruited into action by these thought patterns and stories?

Common expressions demonstrate that many people have observed such mind-body connections.

He was bursting with anger.

She died of a broken heart.

He worried himself sick.

She was scared to death.

These are but a few familiar examples of how we acknowledge in everyday language the powerful impact of thoughts and emotions on health. Medical researchers have made interesting discoveries in recent years about the link between thoughts, emotions, and health.

Anger and Hostility

Redford Williams of Duke University Medical Center is a pioneer in the field of behavioral medicine. His work has led to a much clearer understanding of the connection between hostility and illness, especially the effects of hostility on the human heart.

In the 1960s, cardiologists Meyer Friedman and Ray Rosenman had identified behavioral characteristics that seemed to be present in most of their cardiology patients: constant hurriedness, intense competitiveness, and free-floating hostility. Friedman and Rosenman labeled people with this specific cluster of characteristics *type A* (Hafen et al. 1996).

Williams and his colleagues (1993) focused on the hostility factor in type A people. In one study, they found that over 70 percent of patients with high hostility scores (measured by a widely used psychological test) also had severe blockages of their coronary arteries. In contrast, less than 50 percent of those with low hostility scores had significant blockages.

We now know that hostility is an *independent risk factor* for coronary artery disease. In other words, reducing hostility and anger in your life will reduce your chances of coronary disease.

Current health-psychology research links unskillful management of anger and hostility with a number of other health problems as well. Hafen and colleagues (1996) summarize these findings related to anger and illness in *Mind/Body Health*. They note that prolonged or chronic anger can impact almost any part of the body. In particular, chronic anger can have adverse effects on blood pressure, coronary artery disease, migraine headaches, skin disorders, and even the common cold.

This is everyday anger. In *Anger Kills*, Redford and Virginia Williams (1993) point out the widespread and ordinary nature of this anger: "We're speaking here not about the anger that drives people to shoot, stab, or otherwise wreak havoc on their fellow humans. We mean instead the everyday sort of anger, annoyance, and irritation that courses through the minds and bodies of many perfectly normal people. (p. xiii)"

Worry

Worry is another way thoughts and feelings can affect health. We have seen how worry can be understood as the patterns of thinking driven by feelings of anxiety. Often, the content of the thoughts reflects a person's attempt to cope with or eliminate the discomfort and ill ease present as part of their experience of anxiety.

Hafen and colleagues (1996) report some interesting facts about worry and health:

~ About two-thirds of Americans classify themselves as worriers.

~ About half of that group classify themselves as moderate worriers who worry between 10 and 50 percent of the day.

~ The rest of the worriers report that they worry more than eight hours a day.

⌒ Worry has been related to health problems. These include cardiac arrhythmias in patients who have had heart attacks, increased blood pressure in laboratory animals, and asthma in both adults and children.

⌒ Uncertainty as an aspect of worry is particularly potent and toxic. When people are confronted by situations of high uncertainty, when they do not know what will happen next or how they should act, they can experience destructive feelings of helplessness and frustration. Uncertainty keeps people in a constant state of semiarousal, unable to relax, and the price of this ongoing tension and stress is high.

Staying in the present moment is the key. In an article in *Prevention,* Cathy Perlmutter (1993) quotes Jennifer Abel as saying that to deal with worry, it is important to focus on what's going on right now. Worry is almost always future-oriented, Abel says, "so if we can focus on what we're doing right now—the sentence we're reading, the voice of the person speaking—rather than thinking about what someone might say next, we're better off. (p. 78)"

Attitudes and Beliefs

Besides anger and worry, deeply held attitudes and views of self and the world have been demonstrated to have potent effects on health.

The power of attitude has come under intense scrutiny by health researchers. Of particular importance to your health are thought patterns that shape your sense of personal power and control, your confidence in your ability to handle problems and stress, and your sense of hope and optimism or pessimism about situations you face.

Attitudes and Stress

Why is it that some people handle stress with few problems, while others facing the same stressful conditions fall ill?

Suzanne Kobasa and her colleagues have studied stress and stress reactions in a variety of people, including business executives, attorneys in general practice, and women in an outpatient gynecology setting. The subjects in each of these groups faced roughly the same kinds of stressors, yet had different health outcomes. Kobasa and her colleagues studied the personalities and styles of coping of each group. The studies went on in some cases for as long as five years. In the end, the researchers found a powerful correlation between physical health and certain attitudes and beliefs. *They found no correlation between stressful life events and physical illness.* In other words, what the people believed and thought seemed to make all the difference!

Kobasa coined the term *stress hardiness* to describe the qualities of the individuals who managed stress with few or no significant health problems. The three elements of stress hardiness she found to be crucial are *commitment, control,* and *challenge.*

Commitment here means a deep and abiding interest and involvement in what is happening around you, including yourself, others, work, and a set of important values. In other words, feeling a sense of connection is important.

Control means being confident that you have the ability to cushion the hurt or destructiveness of a particular stressful situation. It does not mean that you have to control other people or all aspects of a situation. Control is the refusal to become a victim. It is the ability to focus on what you can control and not be distracted by what you cannot.

Challenge means having the ability to greet the stressful situation as an interesting opportunity for growth and excitement. This inevitably means also welcoming and accepting change, which is constant, rather than feeling overwhelmed by it.

These findings reflect a common and recurring theme in stress research: The stress itself does not cause illness. How a person reacts to stress is crucial. Your way of viewing and explaining what is happening determines the impact stress will have.

Explanatory Style

How do you explain to yourself what it means when something bad happens to you? Do you view the glass as half empty or half full? Everyone has this tendency to explain the unpleasant or "bad" events of their life. The basis of each person's explanation lies in his or her deeply held views or ideas. These ideas form a person's *explanatory style.*

A pioneer in the understanding of the impact of explanatory style is Martin E. P. Seligman of the University of Pennsylvania. In his studies, Seligman observed that how people explained the "bad" things that happened to them had a powerful effect on their health and wellness. Many others have added to this work, including Yale surgeon Bernie Siegel, Charles Carver at the University of Miami, and Michael F. Scheier at Carnegie-Mellon University (Hafen et al. 1996). The results of research in this area of explanatory style indicate that, in truth, we are what we think.

Pessimists tend to view themselves and most situations negatively. They tend to blame themselves for all "bad" events happening to them, and they tend to *catastrophize,* or inflate every situation into the worst thing imaginable.

Pessimists have worse health outcomes, and the correlation is so strong that the pessimistic style actually has predictive value. In other words, researchers have been able to predict which members of a study would have negative health outcomes based solely on their style of viewing life events pessimistically.

Optimists tend to see the good in situations, expect things to go their way, see controllable aspects to situations and focus on those, resist giving up easily, and avoid blaming themselves for what has happened.

In contrast to pessimists, individuals with an optimistic style have repeatedly been shown in studies to have better health outcomes. It is even suggested that having an optimistic style can actually protect you from getting sick.

Wielding the Power of Thought

The majority of this research in attitudes and health points to an important conclusion. The attitudes and views that so powerfully impact an individual's health are learned and can be changed.

When you recognize and understand the attitudes, views, and emotions operating within you, you gain the power to evaluate and change your attitudes. While this change can take time and varies from person to person, the message is clear. You can be a healthier person by recognizing and managing the power of your own thoughts and emotions!

How Mindfulness Can Help

Mindfulness is an awareness that is *not* thinking. It is an awareness that is capable of recognizing thoughts and emotions as they occur and does not identify with them. Mindfulness is friendly, nonjudging, allowing, present-moment awareness.

We know that thoughts play a crucial role in fear, anxiety, or even panic. Consider the following anxiety-based thoughts:

What if I cause an accident because I can't handle the machine?

If I did have a panic attack right now, I wouldn't be able to cope.

I am tired all of the time. What if I have cancer and it is too late?

It will be impossible for me to go into that meeting tomorrow because there will be too many people there who are just waiting to laugh at me.

I am not smart enough to do the job the boss just gave me.

Any of these thoughts (or ones like them) can provoke the fear response. The stress reaction is then underway. If the type of thinking that follows is generated from a deeper thought base of a pessimistic explanatory style, self-blame, or poor self-confidence, there is even more fuel for the body's fear system to burn.

Subjectively, it can go something like this. The body's fear system is aroused. The hyperarousal is experienced as somewhat unpleasant. The body and the mind are buzzing. Thoughts get started. They can be worrisome and frightening themselves. The fear system response intensifies. The sense of self, of *I-me-mine,* may grow very strong. It can even feel rocklike and heavy. Sometimes *I-me-mine* feels so threatened that overwhelming panic seems to be all that is present. Annihilation of self, of *I-me-mine,* is the compelling moment-by-moment concern.

That is when mindfulness practice is so important. When you practice mindfulness, you make the decision to stay present and examine your own unfolding inner experience. Attention is poured into your interior landscape. You turn toward fear and anxiety, toward thoughts and sensations as objects of your kind attention. You don't have to fix anything as you pay attention this way. All that is asked is that you bring compassionate attention to what you are experiencing, moment by moment.

You establish attention on the experiences themselves, using an anchor such as the sensation of your breathing to help you stay present. As you open to and observe the body sensations, and the thoughts, and the next wave of sensations and thoughts, and so on, you recognize all of these occurrences simply as impermanent, passing events. A sense of spaciousness and ease arises can and surround the disturbing experiences. You feel calmer and your attention has a sharper focus.

By allowing the thoughts to happen and recognizing them as simply another experience in the present moment, you can stop the cycle of identifying with and reacting to the experiences. It is now possible to connect more deeply with yourself and your inner life as it is unfolding.

From the perspective of the mind-body interaction, now there is a break in your identification with the experience of anxiety—both the physical and cognitive aspects of it. Mindful attention breaks the cycle of thoughts fueling the fear system. It also gives the balancing activity, the relaxation response, a chance to activate. And by breaking the identification with the fearful thoughts, mindfulness supports the natural capacity of the higher cortical centers to contextualize and interpret the situation correctly. They can do their usual job of turning down the fear system by acting on the amygdala.

Keep in Mind

Thoughts are powerful. They can have a helpful or a harmful interaction with the body's fear system and the experience of anxiety.

You can learn to manage the power of your thoughts and their effects on fear and anxiety by learning to be more present and to pay attention on purpose as the experience of thoughts and feelings and body sensations unfolds.

You may not be able to stop your thoughts or control your thoughts. But you can learn not to identify with them and not to believe them automatically. You can learn to recognize and allow your thoughts to happen. When you hold your thoughts in awareness this way, you use the power of mindfulness to manage the power of your thoughts.

Then, whether you can stop the thoughts is no longer so important. Even when anxious thoughts are present, they lose their ability to intrude in your life and to control you. By being present with awareness, you gain new power over the experiences of your own mind and your life itself.

chapter 5

mindfulness and meditation

Everything happens in the present moment. It is in the present moment, the *now*, that you live. All of experience, whether it occurs inside your skin or outside your skin, is happening in this moment. In order to live more fully, to meet the stressors and challenges of life (including fear, panic, and anxiety) more effectively, and to embrace the wonder and awe of life more completely, it is fundamental that each of us learn to connect with and dwell in the present moment.

To teach yourself the art of attention and presence is both a difficult and beautiful undertaking. The habits of inattention and absence are strong, yet the experience of life, moment by moment, is precious.

The Value of Mindfulness

In the 1997 best-seller *Tuesdays with Morrie,* Mitch Albom recounts a series of conversations he had with his favorite professor from college, Morrie Schwartz. Morrie was dying of Lou Gehrig's disease. Mitch visited Morrie every Tuesday. One Tuesday, they talked about death. Mitch asked Morrie why it was so hard to think about dying. Morrie answered,

> "Most of us all walk around as if we're sleepwalking. We really don't experience the world fully, because we're half-asleep, doing things we automatically think we have to do."

> "And facing death changes all that?"

> "Oh, yes. You strip away all that stuff and you focus on the essentials. When you realize you are going to die, you see everything much differently." He sighed. "Learn how to die, and you learn how to live. (p. 83)"

Morrie goes on to tell Mitch that a key to learning how to die is to accept that "you can die at any time." From this truth, Morrie's appreciation for life is strengthened. He tells Mitch, "Because I know my time is almost done, I am drawn to nature like I'm seeing it for the first time.(p. 84)"

In his wise way, Morrie shares with us a deep appreciation of the preciousness of life's moments.

But what of the moments filled with fear and pain? Are they precious also? What is there to be gained from being present in these moments?

In *The Places That Scare You* (2001), popular meditation teacher Pema Chodron tells a story from her childhood about facing pain. Pema was about six years old, walking down a street and feeling "lonely, unloved, and mad, kicking anything I could find." An old woman saw her and laughed. The old woman told Pema, "Little girl, don't you go letting life harden your heart." The lesson for Pema was clear. "Right there, I received this pith instruction: we can let the circumstances of our lives harden us so that we become increasingly resentful and afraid, or we can let them soften us and make us kinder and more open to what scares us. We always have this choice. (p. 3)"

As a human being, you already have what you need to experience the preciousness of each moment. You have the quality you need to open to what scares you instead of hardening into resentment and fear.

Mindfulness is that quality. Mindfulness empowers you to be truly present.

Mindfulness Is to Be Experienced

Mindfulness is a word in the English language. In any word, or concept which the word represents, there is limited understanding. If you read different books about mindfulness, or hear different people talk about it, you will likely hear different definitions. There are different cultural uses of the concept, as well as different words and symbols used to represent it. So from the beginning, you must recognize that simply to talk about mindfulness, to think about it, or to read about it is not adequate to understand mindfulness.

The words we use to convey ideas about mindfulness are only symbols, only a kind of map. The actual experience of mindfulness lies beyond words and ideas. You can only get this experience through your direct practice. In the truth of your own direct practice experience is the real understanding of mindfulness.

Having said this about direct practice experience, however, we can now discuss some ideas about mindfulness that point in the direction of what happens in direct practice.

What Is Mindfulness?

The word *mindfulness* is popping up everywhere these days. Some people seem to confuse it with the word *mindlessness*, which is actually the opposite! Others seem to think being mindful means having a mind that is full of something, or trying to make the mind full of something. All of this talk can make something confusing out of what is actually a simple thing. Let's try now to move toward a more precise and clear understanding of mindfulness, where it comes from, and what we mean by that term in this book.

Webster's *New World College Dictionary, Fourth Edition,* does not actually define *mindfulness,* but does define *mindful* as "having in mind, aware, heedful, or careful" and *mindless* as "not using one's mind, showing little or no intelligence or intellect, senseless, or thoughtless."

Social psychologist Ellen Langer (1989) used the word *mindfulness* in the context of her important work studying the relationship between mind-states and actions in diverse and common human activities. As she points out, however, her work has been conducted almost entirely from the Western scientific perspective.

Langer does not use the word *mindfulness* in the context of meditation practice. She relates this more to Eastern views of mindfulness. In fact, her work on the subject began with the study of *mindlessness,* or the sort of automatic, unheedful behavior which can cause so much difficulty in daily life. She explains how holding fixed views and mind-sets can make us blind to things right in front of us, and how we pay a high price for this.

These definitions and examples of mindfulness are based in the Western cultural perspective, with its emphasis on thinking, mind-sets, and cognitive perception. They are valuable and have some remarkable similarities to the concept of mindfulness presented in this book. However, there is one important difference as well.

Mindfulness Is Based in Meditation

The approach presented in this book is based upon an understanding of mindfulness developed through *meditation.* This meditation-based approach is grounded in a direct experience of attention and

awareness applied to thoughts, as well as to all other facets of experience in this moment. The understanding and the benefits of mindfulness arise directly out of the experience of the person practicing the
meditation. For this approach to help you, you have to actually
meditate.

You teach yourself the art of attention and awareness by developing and maintaining a stable and dependable mindfulness meditation
practice.

There is much in this book to help you start your practice and to
sustain it when the inevitable obstacles and hindrances arise. However,
it is you who must actually do the practice. Reading about it without
practicing will not be very useful.

Meditation Is Inclusive and Accessible

Buddhists have been practicing meditation, especially mindfulness meditation, for over 2500 years, and have amassed quite a bit of
useful information about how to do it. It is this accumulated experience
and wisdom that informs the way mindfulness is taught in this book.

Although the meditation methods in this book do have roots in
Buddhist traditions, the actual practices are quite generic. They
require no special belief system or spiritual or religious views. Mindfulness is not bound to any spiritual or religious form.

Jon Kabat-Zinn, in *Full Catastrophe Living* (1990), offers this definition of mindfulness: "Simply put, mindfulness is moment-to-moment
awareness. It is cultivated by purposefully paying attention to things
we ordinarily never give a moment's thought to. It is a systematic
approach to developing new kinds of control and wisdom in our lives,
based on our inner capacities for relaxation, paying attention, awareness, and insight. (p. 2)"

Experience is your best teacher. Give yourself this experience of
mindfulness by building your own meditation practice.

A Closer Look at Mindfulness

To better understand how mindfulness-based meditation works,
let's take a closer look at the different aspects of mindfulness.

Mindfulness as the Capacity for Accurate Reflection

Mindfulness can be thought of as a capacity for accurate reflection that all human beings possess. Unfortunately, many people do not recognize that they have this capacity or that they could and should develop it. Meditation teacher Larry Rosenberg (1998) speaks to this view of mindfulness.

> We human beings have an extraordinary capacity, which we sometimes take for granted until it is called to our attention: unlike other beings in the world who are living out their lives, we have the ability to be conscious of that process as we do so. Mindfulness is often likened to a mirror; it simply reflects what is there. It is not a process of thinking; it is *preconceptual*, before thought. One can be mindful of thought. There is all the difference in the world in thinking and knowing that thought is happening, as thoughts chase each other through the mind and the process is mirrored back to us. (p. 15)

Mindfulness is always there as a potential, but you may not always (or even often) be using it. It is precisely because you fail to recognize and use this potential to be aware that you miss so much of your life and are so imprisoned by habitual ways of perceiving, thinking, feeling, and acting.

Mindfulness as a Quality

Mindfulness is sometimes discussed as a quality rather than a capacity.

Nonjudgment and Openness

As a quality, mindfulness is said to have certain characteristics, including nonjudging and not interfering, or allowing. Mindfulness is also described as nonstriving, not rejecting, and not denying.

Mindfulness opens to and includes whatever arises, just as the mirror reflects whatever comes before it. Mindfulness is not for or against anything. It doesn't try to add or subtract, to improve or change in any way.

Kindness and Intimacy

Intimacy and kindness are other important characteristics associated with mindfulness as it is practiced and developed through meditation.

Rosenberg (1998) recalls the thirteenth-century Zen teacher Dogen, who described the awakened mind as the mind "intimate with all things. (p. 16)" This kind of intimacy means not being detached or separate from what is happening right now, in this moment, but rather being awake, open for the direct experience of life in the midst of it. Practicing mindfulness, you are not aloof or distant but awake and in contact with experience as it happens.

Kindness is a vital characteristic of mindfulness. Many meditation teachers emphasize the importance of having a friendly or welcoming spirit toward whatever arises when practicing mindfulness.

The welcoming spirit of kindness or friendliness helps you to be more open to moment-by-moment experience. It also helps you overcome the deeply rooted habits of judging and aversion that often operate strongly just out of awareness and interfere with your being present and paying attention on purpose.

The popular meditation teacher Thich Nhat Hanh invites his students to smile more when meditating. In his 1987 book *Being Peace*, Hanh tells us that "life is both dreadful and wonderful. To practice meditation is to be in touch with both aspects. Please do not think we must be solemn in order to meditate. In fact, to meditate well, we have to smile a lot. (p. 4)" He continues, "this is the only moment that is real. To be here now, and enjoy the present moment is our most important task."

Facing Pain with Compassion

Intimacy and inclusiveness mean that it takes courage to practice mindfulness. As awareness of what is here grows, the awareness of painful and unpleasant things also grows. It can take courage and endurance to face such pain. This raises the same choice Pema Chodron described: will you become hardened and resentful, or softer and open? Compassion is a willingness to stay present and open to the pain that arises, in the hope that presence might bring relief.

You May Feel Worse before You Feel Better

Because mindfulness practice increases your awareness of and sensitivity to *everything*—including pain and fear—you should be aware that you may actually feel worse in the beginning. However, this is only a stage in the process of healing and transformation. As your meditation practice strengthens, you will learn to relax and stay present even when anxiety, fear, and panic move through the present moment. This is not an act of willpower, but a capacity that you develop through meditation.

Finding Your Core of Openhearted Awareness

One of the fruits of mindfulness practice is the discovery, over time, of the core of steadiness and harmony at your center. This core is dependable, unwavering, and a source of inner peace. Standing at this core, relating to experience—even painful experience—from this place, you have an increased capacity to remain present.

With mindfulness, even the most disturbing sensations, feelings, thoughts, and experiences—including fear, anxiety, panic, and worry—can be viewed from a wider perspective as passing events in the mind rather than as "us," or as necessarily true. By simply being present in this way, you support your own deep healing, and you will discover and dwell more steadily in your own inner space of peace and equanimity.

Meditation teachers often refer to mindfulness as *heartfulness* to reflect these characteristics of intimacy and kindness. Here it is helpful to note the limitations of the English word *mindfulness,* with its emphasis on mind and thoughts. Consider that the character in Chinese that means *mindfulness* has two parts: the upper part means *now,* and the lower part means either *mind* or *heart.*

From this perspective of heartfulness, perhaps another word for mindfulness might be *presence.* To practice presence means to be here with the essence of your being. When you are not here, are distracted, you are *essentially* not here. So to be mindful means to be here with openhearted awareness, essentially and completely, in the present moment.

What Is Meditation?

As I am using the term in this book, mindfulness is developed through meditation. Before going further it is therefore important to be clear about what meditation is and how that term is used in this book.

Meditation teacher Christina Feldman (1998, p. 2) offers a valuable insight into the meaning of meditation practice: "There are several core principles which run through all meditative disciplines. Attention, awareness, understanding, and compassion form the basic skeleton of all systems of meditation."

Attention is "the means of establishing ourselves in the present moment."

Awareness "develops a consciousness that is light, unburdened, sensitive, and clear provides an inner environment that is intuitive and still."

Understanding "is born of the direct and immediate perception of our inner and outer worlds." It provides "the possibility of traveling new pathways in our lives and is part of the tapestry of deepening wisdom."

Compassion directs our kind, nonjudging attention to ourselves and then extends it to every living thing.

Thus, meditation can be understood as a process of transformation involving

⁓ directing attention in a calm and steady way

⁓ developing an awareness that is light and clear

⁓ growing understanding and wisdom about yourself and life

⁓ having the embedded qualities of kindness and compassion

There are literally thousands of ways to practice meditation. As it has been developed as a spiritual practice, the purpose of meditation has been to transform and awaken us as human beings. Through practice, experiential learning occurs. This informs and inspires transformation and awakening. The practice of meditation is equally powerful as a way to transform your experience of anxiety, fear, and panic.

The many different meditation practices may be grouped into two general categories: concentrative practices, which emphasize single-pointed or narrow attention, and mindfulness practices, which emphasize awareness or mindfulness. As we'll see, mindfulness practices are uniquely suited to addressing fear and anxiety because they emphasize taking a different approach to fear and anxiety in the present moment.

Of the four major methods of meditation researched in the past twenty-five years or so by Western medical science, three (transcendental meditation, respiratory one method, and clinically standardized meditation) emphasize the concentrative approach. Mindfulness meditation is different in that it emphasizes awareness.

Mindfulness benefits from the ability to concentrate or focus attention, but is not the same as concentration. And, in practice, all meditation methods must employ some combination of concentration and awareness. However, knowing the difference in emphasis between concentrative and mindfulness approaches will help you understand why mindfulness meditation is so powerful in managing anxiety.

Concentrative Approaches

To practice meditation in a way that emphasizes the concentration of attention, you would usually take a narrow focus on a single object. The object could be internal or external. The object could be the sensation of your breath, or it could be a sound outside of you. It could be the repetition in your mind of a simple phrase or word.

If the context is spiritual or religious, this phrase might be a meaningful or sacred one, even a prayer. Or, in a spiritual context, you might fix your attention on an external object such as a sacred figure, a painting, or a burning candle. If the purpose and context of the meditation practice is health-based (for instance, to lower blood pressure), then the object of concentrated attention is typically more everyday or neutral, such as the breath sensation or a sound or repeated phrase without specific religious or spiritual meaning.

In practices that emphasize concentrated attention, when the attention wanders or is drawn away from the object, the practitioner gently returns attention to the object. Although the meditator may notice where the attention goes, the practice is not to dwell there, but to return attention as gently and patiently as possible. This must be done literally thousands of times and is viewed as necessary in order to train the mind. It is by concentrating attention that the relaxation response is elicited.

Mindfulness Approaches

The second category of meditation practices emphasizes awareness or mindfulness. Mindfulness meditation involves paying attention in a way so as to be more aware of the present moment and all that is here now, without judgment. Mindfulness is a practice that is not about thinking but is nonconceptual.

Mindfulness builds on your innate capacity for knowing what is here, now, including thoughts. This awareness is cultivated by paying attention on purpose, broadly, deeply, and without judgment of whatever arises in the present moment, both inside and outside your skin. True present-moment awareness is they key to transforming your relationship to anxiety. It allows you to observe your anxious thoughts without judgment, recognize them simply as thoughts arising in the present moment, and maintain a calm center that is not defined by fear.

What Meditation Is Not

With so many ideas circulating about meditation, it is important to consider some of the things mindfulness meditation is not.

Meditation is not "positive thinking." In fact, it is not thinking at all, but includes paying attention to thinking. In mindfulness practice, thoughts become objects of attention just like everything else.

Meditation is not just another relaxation technique. Although it is supported by relaxation and calm, mindfulness meditation is far more than that. Mindfulness meditation seeks increased awareness, and that awareness brings wisdom and freedom from habitual reactions.

Mindfulness practice does not mean going into a trance. You are not trying to leave or change the experience in this moment; you are trying to stay present with it.

Meditation does not mean trying to "blank your mind." By practicing mindfulness, you will become more conscious and will have a deeper connection with yourself and life, moment by moment.

Meditation is not just for priests, monks, and nuns. You don't have to do or be anything special. Meditation is a way of remembering and reconnecting with the natural quality of awareness and presence all humans have.

Meditation is not selfish. *Self-full* might be a better word to describe the changes that come with mindfulness meditation. True, you can neglect your duties and relationships in the name of meditation, but this is a distortion of meditation. As you practice mindfulness meditation correctly, you will become more aware, and others will be more likely to experience you as helpful, present, and compassionate.

Keep in Mind

The meditation practices included in this book are based on the key principles of attention, awareness, nonjudgment, and openheartedness. As we move forward, we will see how this approach can guide us in applying mindfulness, kindness, and compassion to the experiences of fear, anxiety, and panic.

The goal of this book is to help you build and sustain a daily mindfulness meditation practice and bring it forward in your everyday life. As you do that, you will teach yourself to manage fear, anxiety, and panic most effectively.

chapter 6

your attitude
is important

A rose needs certain conditions if it is to flower. Good soil, sunlight, air, moisture, proper nutrition, and protection from pests are some of the key ingredients. Likewise, anyone starting or maintaining a meditation practice needs certain conditions if their practice is to thrive.

A main goal in this book is to help you establish a strong and supportive daily mindfulness meditation practice. Such a practice will help you overcome the powerful intrusion of fear, anxiety, and panic into the routines of daily life.

A successful meditation practice requires both internal and external conditions of support. This chapter is focused on the internal conditions. In the next chapter, we will take a look at the necessary external conditions and some practical issues related to meditation practice.

The Key Factors Within

There are four important internal factors that support your meditation practice.

Attitude. Your attitude about practicing meditation should not be too idealistic or too cynical. The *don't*-know-it-all attitude is best.

Curiosity. Cultivate the interest and desire to discover something more about yourself and your life as it unfolds, even in the unpleasant or difficult moments.

Motivation, determination, and discipline. To benefit, you have to practice mindfulness faithfully and regularly. You don't have to like it, but you do need to do it!

Belief in yourself. This means developing confidence in your own ability and power to do something to help yourself manage fear, anxiety, or panic in your life.

What Approach Will You Take?

Take a moment to consider the inner orientation you are bringing to this practice of mindfulness. The orientation or position you take at the beginning is absolutely critical. It is probably the most important condition of all.

The Cynic

Have you become cynical, even bitter, about your situation? Are you discouraged about ever finding relief? Are you feeling hopeless? Have you given up on the possibility of overcoming the fear and anxiety that interrupt your life?

The cynic might approach the idea of practicing mindfulness for help with fear, panic, and anxiety with an attitude something like this: "I know nothing can really help me, but I will do this meditation anyway and prove it!" Then, the first time fear or panic returns, the cynic says, "See, I told you so. Mindfulness can't help me either."

The True Believer

Or are you the "true believer"? True believers come to meditation practice (like so much else in life) with an idealized view that "this is the answer to all my problems. This will take care of me." They don't understand that effort and practice are required, or that life will continue to present challenges and ups and downs. When fear or panic returns, the true believer becomes discouraged and says, "Oh, well, I guess it wasn't the answer after all. I must keep looking."

The Curious Skeptic

There is a middle ground that is far more realistic and more potent. The most helpful attitude you can bring and maintain throughout your practice is what Jon Kabat-Zinn (1990) has called *skeptical curiosity.* You are not a true believer, and you are not a hopeless and bitter cynic, either.

You are skeptical in that you do not automatically assume that your practice of mindfulness will relieve all your problems or that it will happen without effort and commitment on your part. In fact, you are willing to admit that you do not know how or even if it will really help.

But, at the same time, you are curious. You recognize that any worthwhile pursuit takes commitment, discipline, and effort. You are willing to give your best effort to your mindfulness practice over time to find out where that might lead. You are willing to give yourself and the process some time and energy, and are curious to learn what might happen if you stick with it.

If you want to develop your ability to calm your mind, relax your body, and be truly aware, now, in the present moment, then you must examine your attitudes and be willing to change them if necessary.

Embarking on an Experiential Journey

To cultivate the healing power of mindfulness in your life requires more than just sitting in a meditative posture, or following a set of meditation instructions, or listening to a tape. By taking on this practice, you are embarking on a new way of learning. The focus is on you and your life as it unfolds moment by moment. And this way of learning happens from the inside out.

This is experiential learning. You learn by having the experience directly. As you practice mindfulness, your life continues to unfold, and your practice changes your experience of your life.

What and how much you learn depends directly on you. You learn through your entire being, not just the part that thinks. You learn by being present as experience occurs in your body, through your senses of seeing, hearing, smelling, and tasting as well as what is happening in your thoughts.

This learning takes place only through your own practice and willingness to be present and to pay attention. It is not based on preconceived ideas or what you think you know. Your understanding grows over time as you gain direct experience practicing meditation regularly.

This learning cannot be forced, but is a process of allowing, discovery, and unfolding. The awareness you develop does not try to change anything. Change comes later, and is guided by awareness. It is very likely that you will make significant changes in how you handle fear, anxiety, and panic, but you will do so only after you have touched each of those experiences deeply with mindfulness. Acceptance and openness to what arises in the present moment is vital.

It is helpful to view the activity of meditation and its application to healing your life as a process or a journey. It is ongoing, changing in each moment, and changing over time as you develop consistent habits of attention and presence.

From this view, the attitudes you hold (especially the unrecognized ones), the attitudes you let go of, and the attitudes you cultivate all have a deep impact on the process of learning and being present.

The Seven Essential Attitudes

In *Full Catastrophe Living* (1990), Jon Kabat-Zinn outlines seven specific attitudes that form a foundation for mindfulness. They apply directly, moment by moment and day by day, as you cultivate and deepen mindfulness. These attitudes are *nonjudging, patience, beginner's mind, trust, nonstriving, acceptance,* and *letting go.* Throughout this book you will be called on to recognize and to apply these important attitudes as you learn to cultivate mindfulness and apply it to face fear, anxiety, and panic.

The attitudes support each other and are deeply interconnected. Practicing one will lead to the others.

Your ability to bring these attitudes forward in your mindfulness practice will have a great deal to do with your long-term success and ability to calm your anxious mind. In the actual meditation practices you will learn, you will revisit them many times, and will come to understand what vital supports they truly are.

Nonjudging

Mindfulness is compassionate, openhearted, choiceless awareness. It is cultivated by taking the position of an unbiased, attentive witness to your own experience as it happens in the present moment. To do this requires that you begin to relate to the contents of experience, without judgment, as the present moment unfolds.

The habit of categorizing and judging experiences locks you into patterns of reacting and repeating thoughts, feelings, and behavior. You may not even be aware of these patterns. Judging acts to separate you from the direct experience of each moment and from the unfolding reality of life. When you practice mindfulness, it is important to recognize the judging quality of mind and identify the judgmental thinking as it arises. It is equally important not to judge the judging! Simply note that judging is present.

Bill's Story

Bill has generalized anxiety disorder. He lives with intense worry and imagines a terrible variety of things that could happen in almost every situation he enters. Over the years of his suffering, Bill has come to hate the worry and fears. To make matters worse, he has become a harsh critic of himself in the process. Whenever a fearsome fantasy arises, it is accompanied almost immediately by mean and insulting thoughts like "I am such a weakling" or "I am so crazy."

After Bill began to practice mindfulness, he started to notice the patterns of his thoughts and the habits of criticizing and judging that arose whenever the anxiety and worry came. He remembered to practice nonjudging.

After a while, Bill was able to recognize at least some of the judgments as just another set of thoughts passing through the present moment. He found he could relax a bit, could soften in his mind and body, despite the fact that his anxiety was still intense at times.

Bill also began to notice that he could allow the feeling of anxiety itself to be present along with all the scary thoughts. They happened, but they had lost a lot of their hold over him. He was able to view these events, unpleasant as they were, as something else passing through the present moment.

Patience

Patience is the ability to bear difficulty with calmness and self-control. It requires connection with your calm inner core and also some faith and courage. Patience also requires a degree of kindness and compassion for yourself as you bear the upset of the situation. Often, impatience arises when the *ego*, the self-centered part in each of us, screams for things to be different than they actually are.

There is a certain wisdom that supports patience. This wisdom recognizes that things have a life cycle of their own and that the ego is not always calling the tune. As you learn to rest more and more with this truth, your patience will grow even stronger.

To become more patient, you must learn to recognize impatience. Notice any tendency to rush through one moment to get to the next.

Helen's Story

Helen does not have a diagnosed anxiety disorder. She lives a busy life, holding down a good job while maintaining a home for her husband and two children. She also helps care for her elderly mother, who lives in a nearby town. As her mother's health began to decline, Helen became more worried about her mother's health and ability to care for herself.

About nine-thirty in the evening on a weeknight, Helen got a phone call from her mother's neighbor. He was at the hospital with Helen's mother, who seemed to have had a stroke. The neighbor told Helen the situation was very serious and urged Helen to come to the hospital immediately.

Helen's mind instantly began to fill with all kinds of fear-driven stories and ideas about her mother and what needed to be done. She felt her body begin to tighten up and noticed aches in her back and neck where she usually feels her stress. She was aware of a sinking feeling, and some deep dread began to arise.

Helen had been in a meditation class for a few months before receiving this phone call. She had been learning about mindfulness and practicing some. She had started to pay attention more closely to her breathing, breath by breath. She had acknowledged more deeply the upset and pain in her own mind and body. She had learned to remember the quality of patience. Even while her ego voice was screaming at her, she was able to remember that life moves in cycles of creation and dissolution, and that she would have little or no control over the situation with her mother.

In the moments after the phone call, Helen was able to use the conscious breathing method from her meditation class. She felt more centered. She informed her family, left a message on her supervisor's voice mail, and prepared to leave for the hospital.

As she traveled to be with her mother, Helen stayed present with herself with patience. She continued to acknowledge the fear and dread, the body reactions to the stress, and the cascade of plans and thoughts roaring through her mind. She remained patient with all of this and rested a bit in the wisdom that things are the way they are, and she was doing all she could do.

Beginner's Mind

When you begin to observe what is here in the present moment, the thinking mind tends to believe it knows all about what is happening. Or it tries to control what is happening by desperately seeking more information. The activity of thinking forms as a kind of filter between you and the direct experience and true richness of life as it unfolds moment by moment.

To practice beginner's mind means to open to the experience in each moment as if meeting it for the first time.

Imagine the wonder of a child as she encounters something for the first time. The first smell of a flower, the first drop of rain, the first taste of orange: all are experienced without the intermediate layer of thought or comparison to the past. These moments are experienced just as they are, in the now, directly, as smell or touch or taste, as sound or sight.

In truth, each moment *is* unique. Though you may have experienced a thousand sunsets, you have not experienced *this* particular sunset. The same is true of a lifetime of in breaths, or the hundredth time you taste your favorite dessert. This particular breath and this particular taste have never happened before and will never happen again.

When practicing mindfulness, you are asked to cultivate this same quality of direct experience, receiving whatever arises as a unique and precious experience. To do this is to practice beginner's mind.

Anne's Story

Anne woke in the middle of the night with her heart racing, feeling she was choking, in a sweat. Thoughts about immediate death filled her head. She was having a panic attack. It had happened before. She had had the attacks for over three years and was under psychiatric care for them. She had noticed that they seemed to come more often when she was "stressed out." Just that morning, Anne had told her best friend that her work and the breakup of a relationship after eight months had "really stressed me out."

As the minutes dragged by and Anne felt worse and worse, the thought "I hate these panic attacks" came to her. "This feels like the last one! I couldn't breathe then either. I think I am going to die."

Then Anne remembered what she learned in her mindfulness meditation class. She acknowledged the fear and upset she felt, and the intense physical sensations in her body. She got out of bed and took a seat in the chair where she meditates each day. She focused on her breathing, breath by breath, until she felt a bit more present. She was still experiencing terror, but she was also aware of some space in herself that seemed to be able to contain the terror.

Anne remembered something about beginner's mind; about trying to meet each experience as if for the first time; about how it doesn't help to assume anything about the experience. That the way you talk to yourself about what is happening can actually worsen things. Anne tried to meet the panic attack as if she had never seen it before.

She had learned to bring mindfulness into her body in her class, so she began to pay careful attention to the actual physical, emotional, and mental experience unfolding as her panic attack. She allowed the sensations to come and go, just as she had been taught. It was not easy. She had to come back repeatedly to her breath for a focus.

After a bit longer, the attack passed. Anne was very relieved. She noticed the clock and thought to herself, "It was over quicker than the usual ones. Maybe these attacks *are* different each time. Maybe I can do something to manage them myself using meditation."

Trust

A basic part of learning to meditate is learning to trust yourself and your feelings. You learn to trust that you can see clearly what is actually happening to you.

As you practice mindfulness, you will deepen your awareness of life and your own moment-to-moment experience. You will develop increasing sensitivity and accuracy in discerning what is here now, and what is happening in your own body and mind, as well as what is happening around you. You will learn that you and you alone are the best person to know what is going on inside your own skin and what is happening outside of it. You do not need an expert to tell you these things.

You can learn to pay attention and to be present using powerful capabilities of attention and awareness that you already have. It is important to learn to trust in your own authority to know yourself, rather than to look outside yourself for authority. In this process, you discover what it really means to be your own person and to live life with authenticity.

Mack's Story

Mack is a veteran of the Vietnam War. For almost thirty years, he fought to hold back the memories that intruded on his daily life. His head filled with terrible scenes and sounds, and his body recoiled from these every way it could. He paid a horrific price, but he managed to hold a job and to maintain his second marriage successfully.

Mack began to have more problems with high blood pressure and disturbing dreams. His medications didn't seem to be working as well. His psychiatrist advised him that he "needed to do something" to break out of the cycle he was in.

Mack heard about a mindfulness-based meditation program. He signed up. After about four weeks of meditating daily and opening his awareness in his body and to his thoughts, he began to feel more relaxed. His blood pressure went down, and his sleep got better.

Then, things got tougher. Mack began to have more vivid flashbacks. They were extremely intense and painful. The details were agonizing. He began to question whether he could survive the experiences.

Mack had a talk with his meditation teacher. The teacher reminded Mack that he is no longer in Vietnam. What is happening is happening only in the present moment. The flashbacks are only memories. The body sensations are only reactions, and they will pass.

Mack began to trust that he was in touch with exactly what was happening. He practiced mindfulness faithfully. As he paid more careful attention, moment by moment, he could see the thoughts and pictures arise, feel his body stiffen and react, and then, amazingly, he watched as the entire experience faded and was replaced by something else. His confidence in himself grew immensely.

It was not easy going, however. Mack had to use all of his new meditation skills to remain present during the worst of the flashbacks. He spent extra time practicing meditation to calm and relax his mind and body. He refused to give up or to give in.

After a few more weeks, Mack was visibly relaxed and happier. He told his meditation teacher and his psychiatrist, "I fought those memories for thirty years because I thought they would kill me. Now I know them for what they are. I trust myself enough to take them on, and I know that I can handle them."

Nonstriving

We spend so much of our lives doing things and trying to change things. This habit of *doing* often carries over into meditation, and it can be a real problem. The ego mind wants to get more of what it likes and wants to get rid of what it doesn't like. When it decides you aren't the way you should be, the ego mind even puts on the pressure to change *you.*

This pressure to do and to change is felt as striving, or straining to be different, to go elsewhere, or to do something else.

The practice of mindfulness involves simply paying attention, without judgment, to whatever is happening. In this sense, meditation is a unique human activity. Meditation is about nondoing instead of doing. To practice meditation is to practice being, not doing.

When you feel a sense of striving or of trying to change things, notice that without judging yourself. In a deep sense, the practice of mindfulness is about truly relaxing, allowing whatever is happening to happen, and bringing clear, compassionate awareness to it as it happens.

Meditation involves a paradox. The best way to achieve your goals about meditation (whether they be control of anxiety and panic, stress reduction, spiritual growth, personal development, or anything else) is to back off from striving for results and instead start to focus carefully on seeing and accepting things as they are, moment to moment.

Jackie's Story

Jackie is a worrier. She introduces herself that way at parties sometimes. But it is no joke to Jackie. Although she has never talked with a doctor about it and she has no diagnosis, Jackie wonders sometimes if her worrying isn't a bit more severe than normal.

She worries about what can happen in practically every situation she faces. She especially worries about work. Jackie is single and has a demanding job with a lot of responsibilities. She often works overtime or steps in for others who are sick or on leave. Jackie is well liked by her coworkers, and many people depend on her. But she finds it nearly impossible to leave work. In the evenings, on weekends, even during vacations, she often worries about people and situations at work.

A few months ago she began to notice that she was even more keyed up than usual and felt tired more often. Some of her friends said she was more irritable, and she felt tight in the neck and shoulders almost every day.

Jackie heard about a stress-management program through a notice at work. In order to participate, she would have to meditate for an hour every day for eight weeks. Although she didn't know how she could possibly find an hour each day to meditate, she decided to try it and see if her worry would stop.

Jackie joined the class and began to meditate. She did not do a full hour every day, but surprised herself at how much she did do. She began to experience some relaxation in her mind and body. Her muscles didn't ache quite so much, and her sleep improved. She even thought she had a bit more energy at work.

In class one night, the teacher talked about how much people strive and strain, and how meditation is about just *being*. Jackie began to notice how that applied to her. She reflected on how much she felt she took on the responsibility to change things in everything she did. She began to notice this attitude more and more on the job, and began to allow herself to feel it without identifying so much with it.

Jackie made an interesting discovery about herself in meditation. While she was meditating, she began to notice how much she felt a restless tension in her body. The more she paid attention to this, the more she could begin to hear thoughts of criticism and urgency in her mind. She began to try to just let things be, as her teacher advised.

The restlessness in her body seemed to ease, but the thoughts got meaner. Jackie kept practicing. She even stopped trying to make the thoughts go away or change. As she just let the thoughts "chatter on," they began to quiet.

Jackie had succeeded in being and not-doing. She stopped *trying* to stop worrying and, in that way, became free from worrying after all.

Acceptance

The process of acceptance begins with the willingness to see things exactly as they are in the present moment. Can you keep your attention focused exactly here and now, taking each moment as it comes and connecting with whatever presents itself?

Often, to be able to accept what comes into awareness, you must pass through periods of intense feelings such as anger, fear, or grief. These feelings themselves require acceptance.

Acceptance means seeing things exactly as they are rather than as you think they are or as you think they should be. Remember, things can only change in the present moment. You have to see things as they are and yourself as you are—truly—in this moment if you wish to change, heal, or transform yourself or your life.

Acceptance includes softening and opening to what is here. The sense of struggle is released. By ceasing to deny and to fight with the way things are now, you can find yourself with more energy to heal and to transform what is here.

Acceptance does not mean you have to like everything or that you have to take a passive attitude. It does not mean you have to be satisfied with things as they are, or that you have to stop trying to change things for the better. As we are speaking of it here, acceptance simply means willingness to see things as they are, deeply, truthfully, and completely. This attitude sets the stage for acting in the most potent and healthy way in your life, no matter what is happening.

Sam's Story

Sam had never liked going to the dentist. As a child he had to have quite a lot of dental work, and it left its mark on him. All he could remember was the pain, the smells, and the sounds as the dentist worked in his tiny mouth. His childhood experience was so damaging that as an adult Sam simply did not go to a dentist.

Then, the day came when he could stay away no longer. He had been having pain in a right lower molar for weeks. Advil and aspirin had lost all effectiveness. Sam was distracted by the pain and couldn't chew easily on that side. His wife did not have this fear of the dentist and made regular visits to her dentist, whom she liked. Sam decided he had to go, and made an appointment with his wife's dentist.

In the dentist's chair, with his mouth open while the dentist did the exam, Sam began to be flooded by the fear and painful memories of his childhood dentist visits. He began to sweat, and his heart raced even faster. He began to wonder if he could go on.

Then he remembered the talk in his meditation class about being relaxed and present, and being willing to see clearly exactly what is here. The teacher had defined acceptance that way. He had invited the class to practice mindfulness by softening and opening in whatever situation or experience they found themselves.

Sam figured he didn't have anything to lose. He shifted his attention away from the memories and thoughts in his head, and concentrated all of his attention on his breath. He used his breath to connect his attention to his mind and body in the present moment. He felt the in breath and the out breath. On the out breath, he felt the sense of relaxation in his body and allowed it to strengthen. Sam began to feel a little better.

He began to let himself feel the different sensations, to hear the sounds, and even to smell the smells. He came back repeatedly to his breath and, whenever he felt his body stiffen, he imagined the breath went out exactly at that spot and brought a feeling of relaxation with it. He was breathing into the experience and staying present with the experience as it was.

The dentist said, "Good news. You just have a small cavity and some gum infection around the tooth. We will fix you up in no time."

Sam remembered more about acceptance from his class. He said to himself, "This is not pleasant, but it is the way it is, and I seem to be managing it better than I expected. I will just keep on trying to be here with things since it won't help to fight them." And he kept on working with his breath and relaxing, paying attention to things as they unfolded.

When the work was finished, the dentist actually thanked Sam for his cooperation.

Letting Go

Letting go, or *nonattachment,* is another attitude essential to mindfulness. Much of the time, people are practicing the opposite attitude, clinging, without even knowing it. Often, what you cling to most strongly are ideas and views about yourself, others, and situations. It is a kind of clinging on the inside. It may be difficult to see, but is easily felt.

These ideas to which you cling filter and shape your moment-by-moment experience in profound ways. When you start paying attention to your inner experience through meditation, you will rapidly discover which thoughts, feelings, and situations your mind seems to want to hold onto. And you will notice other things that it wants desperately to get rid of.

Clinging is driven by liking and disliking, and by judgments about things. As you practice mindfulness, it is important to put aside the tendency to judge each experience. Instead, you teach yourself to *recognize* judging. Don't get caught up in good or bad, high or low, pleasant or unpleasant. Just let your experience be what it is, moment by moment.

This *letting be* is actually a way of *letting go.* By not interfering, by just letting things be, you give them a better chance to go.

Can you feel the sense of contracting and hardening that arises around both pleasant and unpleasant situations? Letting go just means releasing the contraction around the thing and allowing it to be. It is not necessary to push the thing away. No force is required. Just soften the contraction. Just let go. You do it all the time, actually. Make a fist. Squeeze it tight. Now let go. Notice the feeling. Try it again. This is the physical sensation of letting go. Practicing meditation, you are practicing letting go on the inside. Become familiar with the interior sense of contraction, in the body and the mind. Then practicing letting go of that.

Alice's Story

Alice is troubled by an irrational fear. She knows it is irrational. She has lived with it since her teenage years, and yet, at age twenty-eight, she still experiences it frequently. She recently read a magazine article about social phobia and thought it described her perfectly.

Alice's fear usually has to do with the irrational idea that she will embarrass herself in some way in front of others. She is tormented by thoughts that she will do something "stupid" or "crazy" in public and be humiliated. This fear has led Alice to avoid situations with others, especially social situations involving strangers. On occasion, she has declined job opportunities if they involved public speaking or making presentations to large groups.

Alice knows her fear is out of proportion to the situations of her life. She is quite intelligent and did well in school. She has some good friends, but sometimes feels she must decline their invitations because her fear of embarrassing herself is so strong.

The article Alice read mentioned that learning relaxation skills and meditation might help some people with social phobia. She decided to find a meditation class and see if it could help.

Alice joined a mindfulness meditation class taught at a local hospital. As she began to meditate, she recognized the powerful interaction of her mind and body. She learned to connect with her body and to relax her body simply by paying attention to the parts, something her teacher called the *body scan.* Then she was amazed to notice how having just one or two of the fearful thoughts about humiliating herself in public would cause her body to stiffen and her heart to race.

She heard the teacher explain that letting go is important and that sometimes the only way to let something go is to let it be. Alice decided to practice doing that with the irrational fears that were disrupting her life. Whenever she had the thoughts about public embarrassment, she just listened. Even though they continued to frighten her, she tried to let them just be there, in her awareness, without doing anything about them. After a while, Alice could see the thoughts in a wider and softer way. She didn't think of them so much as her enemies anymore, but as just some passing noise. Alice began to think she might be able to accept more of the invitations from her friends.

Keep in Mind

In this chapter we have learned about the important inner conditions and attitudes that form the foundation for your mindfulness practice. Meditation will be most effective if you approach it as a curious skeptic, motivated to practice and confident in your innate power. Mindfulness is founded on the seven essential attitudes of nonjudging, patience, beginner's mind, trust, nonstriving, acceptance, and letting go. Recognizing and cultivating these inner qualities will create the optimal conditions for you as you teach yourself to be present in order to manage fear, anxiety, and panic.

chapter 7

building your
practice
foundation

Although the internal conditions—attitudes and habits of think-ing and feeling—are crucial elements of support for your mindfulness practice, there are external conditions and issues that deserve your attention as well. If you are to have a reliable medita-tion practice, you need a strong foundation.

Where you do your formal meditation practice and when you do it, having the support of those you live with, gently reminding yourself to return to the present moment in different situations, and the skillful use of readings, tapes, and other guides are all elements of a strong foundation for meditation. You will also want to consider things that might be hindering your practice.

Formal and Informal Meditation Practice

In this book, and generally in mindfulness-based meditation, we talk about *formal meditation* and *informal practice*.

Formal meditation is the period of time when you practice meditation as your main activity. I recommend you do a mindfulness practice as a formal meditation at least once daily for at least thirty minutes.

Informal practice means that throughout the day, in different situa-tions, you practice mindfulness of what is happening. You can pay attention on purpose to the activity itself, or use conscious breath-ing as a way of establishing contact with the activity and linking mind and body in the present moment.

The suggestions in this chapter will help create the best possible conditions for your formal practice of meditation. Your informal prac-tice of meditation will flow naturally from your formal practice.

Supporting Your Formal Practice of Meditation

Let's look more closely at the external conditions, along with some practical suggestions to optimize the support that each can provide you.

Where to Meditate

It is important to make an actual place in your physical environment for meditation. The idea is to avoid having to decide where to meditate each time you want to do your meditation practice. This will help make meditation a routine in your life, which is what you need for it to actually help you.

Pick a comfortable chair or cushion in one room in your home and let that be the usual place you practice. Of course, you can go outside or use another place at times, but having a designated spot is a great support. Some meditation traditions refer to this as *the one seat.*

You will be more inclined to meditate if the room is inviting. Make it beautiful. If there is clutter everywhere, and that distracts you so much that your mind spins story after story about cleaning up the clutter and all you have to do, then do something about the clutter and keep the area clean.

Include some personal items that help create a sense of security. This will help you feel safe as you challenge yourself to remain present when fear or anxiety arises.

It helps if your beautiful, safe place to meditate is also reasonably quiet. While it is not necessary that you have absolute quiet around you (indeed as your practice grows you will learn how to work with all kinds of sounds and distractions), it is a good idea to let your phone or pager ring in another room and to turn off the TV, radio, computer, CD player, or whatever else is in the background.

It is often said that the world around us, the outer world, accurately reflects the world within us, the inner world. And, to some extent, having a peaceful outer world can help you reconnect to the peace and calm within. You can take advantage of this relationship between the inner and outer world explicitly as you set up the place where you meditate each day. Let the inner world of peace, calm, and beauty show itself in how you establish the physical place where you do your meditation practice.

When to Meditate

In the same way that you need to make a place in your home to meditate, you need to make a place in your schedule. When are you most likely, each day, to have the time and the energy to do your meditation? The goal is to establish a habit of meditating, like the habit of brushing your teeth. Pay attention that the time you choose enables you to practice almost every day at about the same time. Don't be too rigid, however. First thing in the morning or midafternoon or early evening could be just fine. You probably cannot practice at precisely nine in the morning or three in the afternoon or seven-thirty at night every day. Choose a time when, for the most part at least, you will not be interrupted by outside demands or by other people.

Wakefulness is important. The time you pick to practice meditation should be a time when you have enough energy to practice. Some people try to practice just before they go to bed. Then they find they are too sleepy to meditate! It can be helpful to do some meditation before going to bed, but if you find yourself repeatedly falling asleep or feeling too dull and drowsy to pay attention, try another time of day.

You will need to experiment to discover the best way to bring meditation into your life. If there is a time of day when you feel particularly anxious, you might try meditating then. If you do so, consider also meditating at a time when you usually feel less anxious and can more easily gain perspective on the anxiety without danger of becoming lost in it. Remember that the practice is to hold the experience of anxiety in the focus of mindfulness.

Developing Your Own Program of Daily Meditation

With place and time established, you will want to consider your program of practice. What should you do during the meditation time you have now created?

In this book you will learn several methods of meditation, all aimed at developing mindfulness. *Awareness of breathing, choiceless awareness, body scan, walking meditation,* and *loving-kindness* are the formal meditation practices you will learn. The emphasis is slightly different in each one.

I recommend that you begin with two to three weeks focusing on awareness of breathing, body scan, and walking meditation. (If you happen to already have a yoga practice, you can continue doing it mindfully in place of the walking meditation. Both yoga and walking meditation are *body movement practices.*) In weeks four and five, begin the practices of choiceless awareness and of loving-kindness.

In general, you should do some *sitting meditation* and some *body-focused meditation* each day. Sitting practices include the awareness of breathing, choiceless awareness, and loving-kindness. The body-focused practices include body scan and walking meditation (as well as yoga, which is outside the scope of this book).

People often manage this by doing about twenty to thirty minutes of sitting practice plus another twenty to thirty minutes of body-focused practice each day. They often split these up into two different practice sessions.

After about six weeks of practice, you will be ready to develop your own schedule for practice using the different methods. This calls for experience with the different practices, and for recognizing your own resonance with a particular one. Some people choose to deepen the practice method they felt most at home with, while others spend at least some time working on a method they found more difficult.

It is very important to stick with whatever practice you choose. A good program would be to do the same sitting practice daily (at least five to seven times a week) for at least two to four weeks. The same commitment is good for the body-centered practice. Try to avoid "sampling" one, then the next, without really digging in and experiencing a single practice deeply.

As you actually do the practices in this book, you will develop a feel for them and how they fit for you. Your goal is to experience growth in your capacity to be present with clarity and openness. Each of the different practices offers something valuable to help you.

If you like, you can use the meditation instructions in chapters 8 through 12 as scripts to make a tape or CD to practice with. Remember to read slowly and to pause a few breaths between each section of the instructions.

Being a Gentle Reminder for Yourself

Bringing mindfulness into your life is a kind of training of the mind and heart. Like any other training, it takes some work. Effort, energy, and discipline are required. You can help yourself by taking a patient and gentle attitude. By being a gentle reminder to yourself, being a friend, essentially, to your own practice, you will find powerful support and assistance opening to you as you meditate daily.

Overcoming Resistance

Encouraging yourself to practice formally, especially when you don't feel like it, can make all the difference in establishing a regular practice habit. First, just recognize the resistance that is present. Then, try to be kind and patient with yourself if you don't feel like practicing. At the same time, you must be firm, like a good parent, or encouraging, like a good friend, so that you do continue to meditate despite the habits of resistance, which everyone faces and must overcome.

Cultivating Informal Practice

It is very helpful and important to develop your informal practice of mindfulness by reminding yourself throughout the day to be present. For example, you might stick a little note with a single word such as *remember* or *breathe* in places where your daily routine takes you: the bathroom mirror, the phone, the refrigerator, the dashboard of your car, or your computer monitor at work. When you see this word, simply remind yourself that you are alive. Return to presence by paying attention to your breath and your body for a few moments without striving or judging.

Keeping a Journal

A final suggestion is to keep a log or practice record. By noting what you did each day and any questions or problems you faced, you can support the development of your meditation practice. Many people like to record the actual number of minutes they practiced and which practice they did. Over time, this provides a point of reference and a foundation for deepening your practice.

Enlisting the Support of Others

The support of the people you live with is especially important. They do not have to meditate with you, or even at all, but it is important that they respect your choice to meditate. This support ranges from not dismissing or demeaning what you are doing to helping more actively by maintaining relative quiet during your practice time or taking care of children, pets, or other responsibilities long enough for you to have time to meditate.

Finding other people to meditate with, at least some of the time, is also a powerful support. People often comment about the increased strength and clarity they feel when meditating with even one or two friends. If you have this support even once or twice weekly or monthly, it can be a great help, especially in difficult times when your own meditation practice feels shaky or fragile.

Counseling or Other Professional Support

Meditation is not the same as counseling or psychotherapy. Meditation is not a substitute for counseling or psychotherapy, either. Today, many professional counselors and therapists are encouraging their clients to learn and practice some form of meditation as part of the process of therapy, and there is a growing interest in how these two processes can work together.

Many people who take up mindfulness practice are not in any sort of counseling relationship, nor do they need to be. However, professional support may be particularly helpful when you are learning meditation to address anxiety or panic. By practicing mindfulness meditation, you are inviting whatever is inside to come out. Meditation is a very inclusive practice. This is a key element of the power of mindfulness to heal and transform you.

But a price comes with this. You have to expect that you may actually feel *more anxious* at times as your awareness grows. You may begin to connect with pain, old wounds, grief, or fears that become so intense that you would benefit from the help of a professional counselor or therapist. There is no shame in this. Be prepared to recognize this if it happens to you, and take the appropriate next step.

Meditation and Prescribed Medications

Some prescription medications can work against your meditation practice by making you too drowsy or too restless. If you find this is the case, consult with your prescribing physician and work to try and reduce these disruptions. It is important that you do all you can to enable yourself to be present and alert.

Many people take up mindfulness-based meditation with the hope of actually stopping or reducing their medications. This is a worthy goal and is realistic for some people. However, you should not stop or change how you take your medication without first consulting with your physician. As your meditation practice grows and strengthens, you may well be able to reduce or even discontinue a medication. As you feel able to do this, be a good partner with your physician by asking the safest way to proceed.

Readings, Tapes, and Other Meditation Guides

There are thousands of books, tapes, and videos about meditation. In using these, it is important to recognize the context and message of the material. You may have already discovered that different aids can give what appears to be directly conflicting advice. In using any such aid skillfully, it is important to remember that meditation must be experienced and that you must do it for yourself.

Mindfulness is about being present with openness and clear awareness of whatever is here. Sensitivity and clarity grow over time with your practice of meditation. The goal of any aid is to help you develop this quality of awareness, often by emphasizing a particular aspect or factor useful in practice. Keep in mind that a particular aid with its specific set of instructions is only one way, not *the* way.

Different meditation teachers often give somewhat different instructions or emphasize a different aspect of the instructions. If you work with different meditation teachers, books, and tapes, you will probably notice these variations. Do not take anyone too literally. Instead, try to understand the essence of what is being taught. Do not let minor variations in instructions or wording throw you off in your own practice. Learn to stand strong in your own mindfulness practice by your own direct experience of wakefulness and presence.

Your goal should be to build a regular meditation practice that does not depend on any tape, book, or script. As you gain meditation practice experience—as you learn through your own experience—you will become less and less dependent on such guides. However, you will probably always find it valuable to continue to read and try on different ideas and practice instructions in your meditation practice. In this way, your practice stays alive and supports your own growth and transformation.

Deepening through Intensive Practice and Retreats

The habits of inattention and absence are strong. They are culti-vated by our tendency to be busy every waking hour. Practicing meditation an hour or so each day is a powerful way to begin to break the habits of inattention and to replace them with habits of presence. Longer, more intensive periods of meditation can also be very helpful in deepening practice.

Many meditation centers offer daylong retreats at which everyone practices meditation and mindful movement. These retreats are usually conducted in silence, and provide a powerful taste of the levels of stillness and clear awareness that are difficult to access in the rush of daily life.

This form of intensive meditation practice is worthy of your con-sideration. As your practice experience grows, you might experiment with longer periods of meditation and mindful movement. For exam-ple, you could do a single two-hour session or a half day devoted to meditation and movement. At some point, you could try a full day. Somewhat later, you may want to consider a weekend or even a weeklong meditation retreat.

In any of these longer and more intensive experiences of medita-tion, you would be wise to work with an experienced teacher. Fortu-nately, there are a growing number of retreat centers and other facilities offering teacher-led retreats.

Possible Hindrances to Meditation

In order to have success with your mindfulness meditation practice, it is important to examine areas of your life that may be especially pain-ful or difficult. Use of alcohol or other drugs or ongoing trauma or tox-icity in a relationship or other situation deserve particular attention.

Use of Alcohol and Other Drugs

It is practically useless to meditate if you are under the influence of any intoxicant. Your meditation practice should not be clouded by the effects of alcohol or other drugs. Take the time to look carefully at your own life. If you have started using alcohol or drugs, or increased your use, consider honestly the effects on you, your relationships, work, finances, and literally everything else. Complete abstinence is not required, but when alcohol or other drugs are interfering with your life, the interference must end before meditation practice can truly help.

Ongoing Traumatic or Toxic Situations

Meditation is not a magic cure. Beginning to meditate can be a powerful stabilizing factor in your life, but if you are living in an ongoing situation that is dangerous or otherwise traumatic or toxic to you, do not expect all of that to change just because you started meditating! What changes as you meditate is *you*. How you respond, how you feel, how present and aware you are.

It is very common for people who begin meditating to make significant changes in the circumstances of their lives—after a while. This action comes as the result of stopping and paying close attention to their own circumstances and their own reactions in those circumstances. It may help to remember that mindfulness is about being, not doing. By being more present, the doing becomes wiser. You could say that *being informs doing.*

So if you are in a toxic situation, *you* may have to change before significant change happens in the situation. However, these situations are similar to the ones involving alcohol, drugs, or medication side effects. If the toxic situation is so disturbing that it actually interferes with your meditation practice, you may have to make a determined effort to take care of yourself first so the meditation can have a chance to help.

Keep in Mind

For meditation to help you calm your anxious mind and live the life you deserve, these internal and external supports are vital. As you learn to handle skillfully the internal attitudes, the external conditions, and some difficult but common obstacles, you will begin to realize the profound power of mindfulness in your life. Remember to remain kind and patient with yourself and what you encounter. In this way, you will deepen your meditation practice immeasurably.

part 2

practicing
mindfulness

chapter 8

mindfulness in
everyday life

Everything happens in the present moment, yet how many of your moments go unnoticed?

Each breath is precious, supporting life moment by moment, yet how often is your attention elsewhere as the breath rises and falls in your body?

Your thoughts are not you, yet how much of your attention is spent in repeating stories and thought patterns while life goes on around you?

Does fear, worry, or anxiety intrude into your awareness, distracting and separating you from the unfolding experience of your life?

As human beings, we have all answered yes to these questions at one time or another. You are not different from anyone else in that regard.

We develop habits of inattention, distraction, and absence over years. Endless busyness and hurrying weaken our concentration and ability to connect deeply with things.

Modern culture encourages us to practice *not* being present. As a result, it is to be expected that teaching yourself to be more present will take some energy and determination. It takes a commitment on your part, and daily effort.

You already have what you need to be more present in your life. The power of mindfulness is in you now. To realize that power requires that you begin to pay attention more closely and with the essential attitudes of nonjudging, patience, beginner's mind, trust, nonstriving, acceptance, and letting go. Your mindfulness will grow stronger as you practice it. In addition to formal meditation, it is very important to practice mindfulness informally in the ordinary activities and experiences of daily life.

As you develop your practice of mindfulness, this apparent separation of formal and informal practice will begin to fade. A stronger sense of presence develops within, regardless of outer circumstances. This strengthened capacity to be present will empower you to overcome fear, worry, and anxiety when they appear. It will also empower you to experience more fully the richness and joy in your own life.

A good place to begin practicing mindfulness is in the everyday activities of life. To be more present, you can begin by paying attention to the things you would not and do not usually notice:

The sensation of this breath going in and out

The feeling of pressure or contact of your back against the chair

The sound of a car passing outside on the street

The smell of your food just before it goes into your mouth

The taste of the *third* and *fourth* bites of your sandwich

The way shadows fall on your table from the afternoon sunlight

This list could go on and on. It is literally endless. The point is that so much of life is unnoticed that not noticing has become a habit.

To build a new habit, a habit of being present, you only have to begin to pay attention to what is already here. It is simple, but not easy!

How you pay attention is crucial. Pay attention *mindfully*. This means noticing without judgment and without trying to make anything happen. Stop trying to change things. This attention is *allowing*. There is curiosity. There is beginner's mind. There is not-knowing (not telling a story about it, not thinking you already know what is here because you have a lot of thoughts about it).

As you approach life this way, being more sensitive to the details of daily experience, paying attention on purpose, you are training your mind to be present. You are awakening to the experience of living fully. You begin to discover the spaciousness and stillness that is inside. This spaciousness can begin to support you. It is there for you in managing fear, panic, and anxiety. It will be there for other demanding visitors like anger, grief, or despair, as well.

The Joy of Being Present

A woman in a meditation class I once taught told me a lovely story about being present.

> *I have been going to services at my church every Sunday for years. I love the music and have heard all the hymns so many times that I feel like I know them all. But yesterday was different.*
>
> *Since I have been in the mindfulness classes, I have learned to be more present for everything. Well, it really worked for me yesterday!*
>
> *At church Sunday, I was worried about some things. But I just stopped and began to focus on my breathing like we do in class, and on my body sensations. After a few minutes, I felt calmer. Then the choir started on one of my favorite hymns.*
>
> *I must have heard that one hymn a thousand times over the years, but this time it was different. It had*

*never been so beautiful. I just listened. I really listened.
And I really heard it: the organ, the voices, the words,
all of it. It was so beautiful!*

*I realized afterward that I had never been so present
before. I had always been caught up in my thoughts or
something else. It was wonderful to be present and to
really hear the music!*

This woman's story is an uplifting example of the power of being present. Being present, being more mindful, opens you to the richness of life in unexpected ways.

You probably started this book seeking help with difficult or unpleasant experiences of fear, anxiety, or panic. That is fine, and there is a good chance that if you do the practices you learn in this book, your experience of anxiety and its grip on your life will diminish.

However, now is a good time to recall that mindfulness is more than a technique for overcoming problems. In fact, the more you are able to let go of outcomes and just pay attention to what is here, the more powerful your mindfulness practice will become. That is one of the paradoxes of mindfulness. And one of the rewards is the fresh connection you will make with the everyday threads of your life.

Be here for the beautiful music.

Be here for the wonderful sunset.

Be here for the warm touch of your loved one's hand.

Be here whenever beauty graces your life.

Mindfulness is strengthened through daily habits of paying attention and practicing presence. It is not mysterious or difficult to understand. It does take effort, especially at first.

So please don't be hard on yourself when you notice your mind wanders repeatedly. Don't let frustration or doubt keep you from starting again. Just pay attention *again* to the little things. Relax and pay attention *again*. Keep coming back to the present. Let yourself fully notice what is here.

Mindful Eating

When I teach a meditation class, I often lead a mindful eating exercise at the first class meeting. I do this for several reasons.

First, it demonstrates that mindfulness is a quality each of us already has. Even newcomers to mindfulness discover it right in the very first class.

Second, people usually have some fun with it. Regardless of the serious and even painful problems that have brought them to the class, participants find themselves laughing, or remembering things, or just feeling more alive after the mindful eating. This demonstrates another basic point. By being more present, you are more alive! And you can actually feel it.

Third, by slowing down and paying attention on purpose with an attitude of curiosity and not-knowing, the participant is practicing core elements of the mindfulness approach. This stopping and being with what is here with nonjudging awareness *is* mindfulness practice. The participant gets a powerful lesson immediately in how to practice.

Other valuable lessons are embedded in this exercise. They include realizing that any activity can be the focus for mindfulness, getting a taste of the wandering habits of the mind, and recognizing how easily thoughts and "stories" come between you and the direct experience of the moment.

You can begin your mindfulness practice on this vital element of daily living, eating. You can experience directly the naturalness and availability of mindfulness for yourself. *You* can begin to realize the joy of being present and the power of paying attention on purpose. And you will begin to get to know the wandering, doubt, and distractedness of your own mind! Be friendly and compassionate with yourself and all of these tendencies.

Are you ready? Let's begin.

meditation practice: mindful eating

Mindfulness is nonjudging, nonstriving awareness. It is cultivated by paying kind and careful attention in as much detail and with as much sensitivity as possible. You can apply this attention and awareness to any activity. Eating mindfully demonstrates the natural availability of mindfulness as well as the potential richness in each activity and moment if you can be present for it.

In practicing mindful eating, you simply pay attention to the experience of eating moment by moment. To do this, you must stop everything else you are doing and really pay attention.

guided meditation:
eating a raisin mindfully

1. Select three or four raisins. Hold them in your hand. Sit comfortably and begin to examine them as if you have never seen or tasted a raisin before. Use all your senses. Look at the raisins. What can you discover about the raisins and about eating them? Let curiosity arise in you. Whenever your mind makes up a story about what you are doing, try to let go of that story and return your focus to the raisins.

2. After a bit, select one raisin and pick it up with your fingers. Let yourself feel it. Turn it over and look at it more closely. Try holding it to the light and notice how the light shines through it or not. Take plenty of time. Notice any tendency to feel impatient or bored. Notice any movement of your mind away from the raisin or into a story about it or a story about anything else. Whenever your mind moves away into a story or another focus, be kind with yourself. You have not made a mistake or done anything wrong. Just bring your attention back to the raisin as gently as you can.

3. Bring the raisin to your ear. Rub your fingers across it. What do you hear? Try the other ear. Try different speeds for your fingers. Can you stay present? Does the raisin make a sound when rubbed? Notice any thoughts or judgments in your mind. Kindly and gently let them go. Return to listening to the raisin.

   Take all the time you need. Notice any tendency to rush. Notice impatience or frustration. Be kind to yourself. Gently acknowledge these feelings and return attention to the raisin.

4. Bring the raisin near your nose. Can you smell it? How does it smell? Can you stay present for the smell itself, not getting lost in the story, not making up a story about how you like or don't like what is present? Is the smell earthy,

sweet, sour, or perhaps nothing much? Is it pleasant or unpleasant?

5. Bring the raisin to your mouth, but don't put it in yet. Notice what is happening inside your mouth. Is saliva forming? Where is it concentrated most strongly? Is your tongue moving? Pay attention as carefully as you can.

6. After a time, move the raisin to your lips, open them, and take the raisin into your mouth. Pay careful attention to what happens next. How does the whole raisin feel in your mouth? What else is happening in your mouth? Let the raisin move around some before you chew it. How does that happen? How does that feel? Notice whether there are thoughts going on, or stories, or judgments. Just let them go. Try to keep the focus on the direct sensation unfolding in your mouth around the raisin.

7. When you are ready, begin to chew the raisin. Notice what happens with the first bite into it. What is the taste? Is it sweet, sour, earthy, bitter, or something else? Is it smooth, grainy, chewy, or what? Does the taste change as you chew it? How? Where in your mouth is the taste the strongest? Try to stay present for the changes that happen as you chew. What can you discover about the taste of the raisin and the activity of chewing? Notice how the raisin disappears. How swallowing happens. What is left? Is there still some taste after the chewing and the swallowing stop? Where in the mouth is there taste? Please allow yourself to sit with all that is here now. What do you notice?

8. After a time, bring your attention to the second raisin. As you look at it, you might allow yourself to reflect on what is in the raisin and on the conditions required to bring it here to you now. This is not an exercise in deep or heavy analysis. It is simply allowing yourself to see how the raisin is the product of conditions of sunlight, earth, water, nutrition, and the care and activity of living things, including human beings. It started as part of a grapevine, grew into a grape, was picked, dried, packaged, and brought to a market, where you found it and brought it home and into your hand just now. Reflecting on anything

in this way can help you to see the connectedness and interdependency of things all around you, including things as simple as a raisin.

9. Gently bring your attention back to the second raisin. You have not seen this raisin before. It is not the same raisin as any other raisin you have ever seen or eaten. Notice any tendency to lose interest or to break contact with this raisin because a part of your mind thinks it knows all about raisins or has "been here, done this" before. Can you let that "knowing" mind go? Can you be here with this raisin with the beginner's mind? Can you be at least as focused (if not more) on this raisin as you were on the first? Look at it. Touch it. Listen to it. Smell it. Chew and taste it. Swallow it. Notice it. What do you discover about this raisin-eating experience?

10. Repeat the practice with the third and fourth raisins. Try to be fresh and present with each one. Notice impatience and boredom, or frustration, or doubt, or any form of thinking or mental conditions that separate you from the direct experience of each raisin you eat. In noticing these tendencies, be kind to yourself. When your mind does wander, when stories or judgments or impatience do arise, it is okay. You have not made any mistakes! This is exactly what happens. You are using your mindfulness now. You are noticing what is happening now. Can you practice acceptance and patience with the experience of being mindful now?

Being Present with a Calm Mind and a Relaxed Body

How did you like the raisin-eating practice?

When people first try this, they are often amazed at what they discover about raisins and about themselves.

They may say something like "I didn't know they were so sweet." Or "I don't really like raisins, but now I don't know why." (Or "I do know why!") Or "They don't have much taste until you bite into one."

It is also common for people to get into elaborate stories or just bursts of memories related to raisins, like "I remembered helping my grandmother make oatmeal-raisin cookies at Christmas."

There is no right or wrong about what you notice. The whole point is to establish mindfulness by making the effort to pay attention on purpose and in an allowing, nonjudging way.

The discoveries you make about raisins or anything else in daily life, on the inside of your skin or the outside of it, depend directly on the quality of attention and awareness you develop.

Mindfulness and the Relaxation Response

Did you notice any difference in the state of your mind or body as you went through the exercise? Many people report they feel quieter, more relaxed, and more present after mindfully eating the raisins.

This illustrates another basic principle of mindfulness. When you concentrate attention without striving or judging but with the attitude of curiosity and caring, the relaxation response can arise. This natural capacity to calm the mind and relax the body is wired into each of us.

This calming and relaxing of mind and body is an important element in all meditation practices. A base of calm and relaxed attention in a relaxed body is vital for mindfulness to deepen.

But remember, the ultimate goal in mindfulness practice is not simple relaxation! Mindfulness is about paying attention with sensitive and nonjudging awareness. If fear or worry or anxiety is here, you practice mindfulness by paying attention to it, just like you tasted the raisins. Calm and relaxation support you in staying present, especially with upsetting and stressful conditions like fear, worry, and anxiety.

Invitations to Practice Mindfulness in Daily Life

As a gentle way of growing your mindfulness practice, start to pay more attention to the everyday activities of your life.

Eat a meal mindfully at least once a day. Or eat at least a few bites mindfully. Snack mindfully. If you snack for reasons besides being hungry, pay attention more carefully to what is happening.

Pick a daily activity to do mindfully. This could be brushing your teeth, getting dressed, taking a shower, walking the dog, washing the dishes, or anything else. Slow down enough to notice the various experiences you feel, see, hear, smell, and taste, and notice what your mind is commenting or thinking.

Pay more attention in the different situations of daily life. As you travel from place to place. In meetings or at work. Taking breaks at your work station. In your garden. At sunset. At sunrise. At the gym. Wherever you are, try to taste the experience like you tasted the raisins.

Don't worry if you do not have much time. You have all the time you need. As you start to make time to be present, you will find that the feelings of urgency and low-grade panic that drive your life are only feelings themselves. They arise and change and pass away like everything else.

Keep in Mind

We live in the present moment, yet habits of inattention and absence keep us from living fully and connecting deeply with what is here. By becoming more mindful of everyday activities such as eating, doing chores, or bathing, you can discover a richness and intimacy with life. This intimacy then becomes the base for increasing joy and wonder as you face life's challenges.

chapter 9

establishing mindfulness, breath by breath

Establishing a calm and focused attention links the mind and body to the experience of the present moment. This principle is central to all meditative traditions. In times of fear and great anxiety, it can also be one of the most difficult aspects of meditation practice.

Meditation teachers emphasize that you must train your attention. The tendency of the mind is to wander. In this chapter, you'll discover the benefits of learning to establish calm and focused attention.

Using Mindful Breathing to Relate to Fear: The Balloon Story

Several years ago my wife, Mary, and I were invited by an old friend, Steven, to join his balloon crew at the annual hot air balloon festival in Albuquerque, New Mexico. We said yes enthusiastically. As crew members, Mary and I joined a team of several others, all of whom were needed to handle our balloon.

The basket of our balloon was enclosed by wickerlike material from the floor up to a railing at a height only slightly above my waist. Riders in the basket held on either to one of the four corner rods connecting the basket to the balloon or to the waist-high railing.

Now, to be perfectly honest, I have never been that comfortable with heights. At least not heights where the only thing between me and the ground hundreds or thousands of feet below is a waist-high guardrail. I have no explanation for this reaction in myself. I have learned to work with it over the years, and it has not limited my activities.

After seeing the basket and hot air balloon setup, my first instinct was that I would be wise to remain a ground-based crewmember. However, Steven was very excited, and quite emphatic and persuasive about how much I would like the trip. As a token of our friendship, he offered Mary and me a place in the basket on one of the first flights in the festival. How could I refuse?

The next thing I knew, I was climbing into the basket, Steven was firing the gas heater overhead, the balloon was expanding, and suddenly, silently, we left the ground.

Everything was fantastic for the first few minutes, as the ground fell away and I looked around, feeling the cool air and captivated by the spectacle of other balloons rising in the beautiful Albuquerque dawn. Then I felt the basket move sideways as the balloon caught a wind current. I looked down over the railing and saw the ground crew, the vehicles, buildings, everything, shrinking. Then I felt the first wave of fear arising in me.

My experience of fear was the usual one. There was a feeling of slight dizziness, some weakness in the knees, a sense of my heart pounding, and a tightening feeling in the throat and gut. My hands were already clutching the railing. I didn't want to move in any direction, and wasn't sure that I could.

Around me, Mary and Steven were excitedly pointing at things going on all around us. They moved about easily in the open basket, despite its now frequent slight swinging motion. They implored me to let go of the rail and turn and look in other directions. Steven kept firing the heater, and we rose higher and higher. I could only grin through clenched teeth and turn stiffly to look either way over my shoulder while maintaining my death grip with both hands on the guardrail. I wished I had stayed on the ground, but knew at that point there was no going back.

The realization that I had to cope was actually helpful. There was no choice except to deal with the fear. There was literally no way to get relief until the balloon landed. I remembered that I did have many years of meditation experience and decided that I would likely need all of it! So I began to focus my attention very deliberately and sharply on the experience of my breathing.

Just as I had been taught and had done in my own meditation practice over the years, I let the breath be just as it was and let the situation be just as it was.

I directed my complete attention to the unfolding sensations of my breath, especially my out breath. After just a few breaths, I noticed some relief. I was able to locate the feelings of fear in my body. I was able to breathe in and out with the fear, holding the sensations in the cradle of the breath. I was able to soften some around the sensations and the situation, and could actually begin to see and appreciate the spectacular scene unfolding around me. I started to move about in the basket and began to take more interest in the ride.

I rode quite a distance with fear that morning. In fact, fear came and went and came back again many times. But each time it came, I was able to meet it the same way, using awareness of the breath as an anchor and consciously breathing in and out with the unfolding experience.

Through this practice of mindful breathing, I was able to change my relationship to the fear experience in a fundamental way. I was able to stop relating *from* the fear, or *as* the fear, and instead relate *to* the fear. I began to relate to fear as just another element of my deep inner landscape.

Each experience of fear, intense and disturbing as it was, became just something else floating there inside me in the cool New Mexico sky. Like the clouds that passed us, or the sunlight, or the other balloons, the fear experience itself changed moment by moment. It was not permanent. And it was not *me*.

With my attention anchored on my breath, my mind and body calmed. Calm and focused attention enabled me to hold the fear as an event in my awareness and to notice its passing as well as its coming. After a while, I noticed it wasn't always there. I could pay attention to the ride. Then, when fear returned, it didn't seem so powerful. I began to feel more confident that I could handle the fear, and with that, I began to relax even more. By the time we landed the balloon, I really had enjoyed the ride.

Responding Wisely to Fear and Anxiety

Everything happens in the present moment. The elements of your life experience are happening now, in the present moment. There is always a choice in how you respond. In those moments when the fear reaction is present, in response to a real threat or as anxiety, the habitual and "unmindful" way is to feel overwhelmed and upset, and to react in fight-or-flight mode. In this "unwise" response, the tendency is to relate and to act *from* the experience of the feeling.

You might even come to believe that you *are* the feeling. You might express this feeling of identifying with the fear reaction, thinking you have become the fearful experience, literally by saying, "I am such a coward" or "I am such an anxious person."

Everything else in your awareness in that moment is tainted by the fear reaction. Everything else is flavored by the intense unpleasantness of the fear reaction. You are literally seeing the world, living life, through the filter of fear.

The usual but unskillful reaction is to fight the unpleasantness of the fear reaction or try to flee from it. If you have a name for the fearful feeling, something like *panic attack* or *fear of heights,* you might feel even more helpless or even defective in some way because you have found no effective way to fight or to flee. This named unpleasantness keeps coming back into your inner world despite all manner of treatments and analysis. You may have come to believe this is a condition, a thing, which is stronger than you are.

But, whether or not you have a name for the fearful condition, reacting from the feeling or identifying with it holds little promise of success.

This is an "unwise" response because it is not based in the truth of how things are. In fact, you are not your fear reaction and it is not you. Also, no matter how intense your fear reaction is, it is not permanent. It depends on certain conditions and will leave when those conditions are no longer present.

To have more hope of controlling fear, panic, and anxiety in yourself, you must forge a more skillful relationship to the moment-by-moment experience. This means relating to the fearful experience in a way that allows you to be with it instead of fighting with it or reacting blindly to it. The wise response, the mindful response, is to turn toward the experience with calm and focused attention.

Discovering Calm and Ease by Paying Attention

We have seen how meditation emphasizes directing attention and increasing awareness. Nonjudging, nonstriving, acceptance, letting go, and patience are crucial attitudes in practicing meditation. These attitudes must be practiced with each breath, especially in the intense moments dominated by fear and panic.

The paradox is that the better way to gain control of fear, panic, and anxiety is to practice *being,* not *doing.* You must actually stop trying to control the feelings and instead allow them to unfold in the light of calm and focused attention.

By allowing things to be as they are precisely in the moments that are most intense, you can break free from the old patterns of thinking and behaving that arise when your reactive, habit-driven mind is urging you to do something.

The way to practice being is not by exercising willpower and gritting your teeth. Clenching and waiting is only another way you continue relating from the unpleasantness, though you might think otherwise. You are still in the center of it, fighting and reacting.

The better and more skillful way to practice being is to let go of the fight and change your relationship to the unpleasantness. You can do this by paying attention in the moment in a different way. It is nonjudging, allowing, and nondenying. Mind, body, and experience are linked in awareness. This way is what we have been calling *mindfulness.*

In order to establish mindfulness in the midst of intense unpleasantness and to calm your mind and body, it is usually necessary to start by taking a concentrated focus for your attention.

Developing your capacity to access the deep calm at the innermost level of your being takes effort and patience. Periods of formal meditation, even periods of extended and intensive practice, are important. You can think of meditation as training for the mind. The habits of distraction and inattention that are so deep must be replaced by new habits of concentration and awareness. You only acquire these new habits by actual practice. Practicing leads to the direct experience of your deepest quality of being, a quality that is spacious and secure.

Having a daily meditation practice is crucial. Doing formal and informal mindfulness practices is the way to develop these new habits.

Awareness of Breathing

One of the oldest and most common meditation practices to build concentration and mindfulness focuses on the breath itself. We can call this meditation practice *awareness of breathing, mindfulness of breathing,* or *awareness of the breath.*

Practicing awareness of breathing immediately brings you back to the present moment. With the breath as your focus, the natural ability of the mind and body to calm can arise. Also, very importantly, with the breath as your focus of attention, there is an immediate shift in perspective. You are now capable of taking a different relationship to all the other elements of your life experience present in the moment. It becomes possible for you to see them just as they are. This means that you are able to come into relationship *to* them and are no longer living *from* them or *as* them.

The remainder of this chapter is devoted to the practice of awareness of breathing, both as a formal meditation practice and informally
in situations of daily life. You will find meditation instructions and suggestions for your daily practice.

You will benefit from taking this practice seriously. Practice as if
your life depended on it. You never know when you will find yourself
in a rapidly rising hot air balloon!

meditation practice:
awareness of breathing

This is a simple yet profound meditation practice. The sensation of
the breath is the primary object of nonjudging, allowing awareness.
You practice by simply paying attention on purpose to the direct
sensations of breathing as they arise, change, and disappear. Whenever your attention moves off of the breath sensation, just notice
that and gently escort your attention back to the breath.

Concentrating attention in this way connects mind and body to
the present moment and to a deep inner calm and steadiness. In this
practice, you actually experience the capacity of your mind to be calm
and stable, even in intense moments. The calm and steadiness extends
to the body as you practice. Over time, in both formal meditation periods and informally in daily life, with consistent and regular practice,
you can expect to feel a deeper sense of ease and relaxation in your
body. You will discover a much more grounded and stable present-moment awareness.

With attention established on the breath, you can use this conscious breathing practice to stay connected in difficult situations. By
learning to breathe consciously into and out with whatever is happening, you teach yourself to remain present with calm attention. The
breath is truly the anchor in the present moment.

And, very importantly, from this base of calm and focused attention, your relationship to the moment-by-moment contents of your life
experience actually changes. You can begin to recognize fear, panic,
anxiety, or any other unpleasantness as a condition rather than as an
identity or point of reference. From that realization, everything—your
experiences and what you feel, think, and do—can change for the
better.

guided meditation:
awareness of breathing

1. Take your seat in a comfortable position in the place you choose for formal meditation. Allow yourself twenty to thirty minutes for this practice. Try to minimize distractions and interruptions.

2. Spend the first few moments of your practice period reflecting on the attitudes that form the foundation for mindfulness practice. Mindfulness is about noninterfering, allowing *presence.* Recall nonjudging, patience, beginner's mind, trust, nonstriving, acceptance, and letting go. In the beginning, pay particular attention to nonjudging and nonstriving. Let go of any agenda about changing fear, anxiety, panic, or anything else, and don't try to make anything happen.

3. Place both feet flat on the floor. Do something comfortable with your hands. Sit in a dignified way with your back, neck, and head in good alignment. Sit in a way that promotes alertness and wakefulness. Let your eyes close gently.

4. Gather and collect your attention in the sensations of your body. Notice your feet on the floor, your back against the chair, your hands resting where they are, and your face and head where they are. Allow yourself to feel the heaviness of your body directly. Allow yourself to relax into the support of the chair and the floor beneath you. Let your body ease and settle as much as possible.

5. Bring attention to your abdomen. Allow your abdomen to relax and become soft. Let the abdomen stay soft.

6. Gather and collect your awareness on the sensations of your breath as it comes and goes. Concentrate your attention at the place in your own body where you can feel your breath come and go most easily and naturally. For some this is the abdomen, for others the chest, for others the nose or even the mouth (if you tend to breathe with

your mouth open). Let your attention settle and focus exactly on that place where the breath sensations are easiest for you to feel. If you aren't sure exactly where to focus, the abdomen is a good place to start. Let your attention rest there now. Allow yourself to feel the sensation of the breath moving in the body just as it is.

7. Allow the breath to come and go without interfering or trying to control it. This practice is about strengthening attention and awareness, not controlling the breath. Keep the focus on just this breath. Let go of any thoughts about how many breaths or the next breath or the last breath. Just this breath. If it helps you to focus, you could whisper quietly to yourself *in* on the in breath, *out* on the out breath, and *pause* or *space* for the space between the breaths.

8. Try to remain present for the entire cycle of each breath: in, out, space, in, out, and so on. As your attention strengthens and mindfulness grows, you can begin to notice the beginning of the in breath, the middle, and the end of it. Same for the out breath and the space.

9. Let your attention settle more deeply into the variety of sensations of the breath in the body. Allow the feeling of the rise and fall of the abdominal wall, the actual stretching sensation, to be the focus. Notice the changing patterns of sensation, how each breath is different—some shallow, some deep, some strong, some weak, some rough, some smooth. Meet each breath with beginner's mind, sensing it as if for the first time. In truth, each breath is here once and only once. Welcome it.

10. When your attention wanders away from the breath sensation, do not be surprised. Gently notice where it went. Is it on another part of the body? A thought or series of thoughts? A sound outside someplace? Perhaps fear, or worry, or anxiety? No matter where your mind wanders, with patience and kindness, escort your attention gently back to the place in the body where you are concentrating on your breath sensation. Praise yourself for noticing that your attention has wandered. You have not made a mistake or done anything wrong. This is the habit of every

mind. It will wander. Recognizing when the mind wanders is a moment of mindfulness. It is a part of the training of the mind that you have undertaken.

11. Keep your belly soft. Notice if there is tightening and tension in the body. Allow softening and relaxing as much as possible. Do not try too hard. Do not try to make anything happen. Do not even try to become a "good" meditator. Simply make your best effort to pay attention to the breath sensations with nonjudging, allowing awareness. Let things be. Let distractions go. Return attention to your breathing.

12. Please keep practicing this way until the end of your formal practice period. It is fine to open your eyes now and then to check the time. Just notice if you are checking very frequently. In that case, check the body for tension and the mind for distraction, boredom, or impatience. Try to let them be, and gently return attention to the breath sensation. Continue opening as much as possible and allow yourself to feel the sensations of each breath directly, as best you can.

13. When distractions like fear, anxiety, restlessness, boredom, or sleepiness become intense and demand your attention, gently notice that. Notice any tendency to fight them. Try to let them be. Breathe in and out with them, including the distractions, as you focus on the breath. Allow the distraction. Consciously breathe in and out through it. Or, if the distractions are still too much, you might try and focus more sharply and closely on the breath sensation. Try focusing on a smaller area in the body. Try to feel the sensation in more detail and more continually. In this way, you actually strengthen concentration. You can find a steadiness inside. Be patient with yourself. None of this happens on the first try. The mind wanders. It is a fact. This is a practice that takes some effort and perseverance. You must find your own balance between making just enough effort to be present, and straining and striving too much. Each time you practice will be different. You are learning how to breathe mindfully in different situations: finding your

breath, allowing, and breathing with and through any distractions.

14. When the time has come for the end of your formal meditation practice period, gently open your eyes, wiggle your fingers and toes, and stretch your body if you like. Notice how you feel, then let that feeling go. Do not try to make any single meditation session, or how you feel afterward, the standard for how all others must be. Let the next practice be just that and only that. Let this practice session stand alone. If your mind tends to compare and to judge one session against another, just notice that and let it go. You haven't made any mistakes by comparing. It is the habit of the judging mind. Be easy on yourself. Just let it go.

Suggestions for Practicing Awareness of Breathing

Awareness of breathing is a fundamental formal meditation practice. Through informal practice, it can become an integral part of your experience of being in the world. Both formal and informal practice of mindful breathing will help change your relationship to anxiety.

Formal Meditation Practice

Give yourself at least twenty to thirty minutes for each period of formal meditation. You can do more than that if you wish. This amount of practice will give you time to experience different things in your meditation and allow the mind and body to settle a bit. When you feel resistance to practicing, try to let it go. Keep practicing. Remember, you don't have to like it, you just have to do it!

Try to practice at least five days out of seven. The benefits you get from mindfulness are directly related to your practice. Even if you do not have your usual time to practice, do as much meditation as you can in the time you have. On the other hand, if something happens and you do not practice formal meditation on a given day, do not get discouraged or give up. It happens to everyone. Just begin again as soon as possible.

Build your practice so that you do not rely on written or recorded instructions. It is okay to use these aids to get started, but the actual meditation instructions are not complicated. Eventually, you should be able to practice awareness of breathing without any external supports.

Informal Meditation Practice

Informal meditation practice means literally taking time throughout your day to stop and do the practice in different situations. You will find you can do any and all of the meditation practices in this book either formally (explicitly and primarily for longer periods of time) or informally (explicitly but for a moment here and there, while things are happening). Try this informal practice of awareness of breathing: Stop and breathe consciously. Practice breathing in and out with what is happening. Do it often. Experiment with it. Play with it. Discover the power of attention and presence in your life.

Let go of any attachment to outcome. Don't try to make anything happen or to change anything. Bring a sense of curiosity and exploration to your life and to this practice. What would it be like to pay attention to the breath before, after, or during various situations? Don't judge yourself by anything, especially feelings of calm or relaxation. This is a practice of awareness and attention. Calm and ease might arise, probably will arise, but they are not the primary goal.

Keep in Mind

In this chapter we have introduced and practiced awareness of breathing as a method of mindfulness. By paying attention on purpose to your breath, allowing it, and allowing yourself to feel your breath in different situations, you can break the habits of reacting and instead connect with your experience in a way that brings you freedom.

Try to think of this practice of awareness of breathing as your friend. Bring it into everything you do. You don't need to think of it as a chore or assignment. You are already breathing. Just start to pay attention more often to what is already happening.

chapter 10

mindfulness
of the body

When aroused, the body's fear system, acting through the amygdala, gives your mind and body quite a jolt.

Muscles contract, leading to feelings of tightness in the chest and throat, along with the fear of not being able to breathe. The heart begins to race. Breath becomes rapid and shallow. You sweat profusely, and tremble and shake. Sugar is released into your blood from body stores. Thinking becomes confused, slowed, or speeded up. Thoughts focus on frightening and disturbing subjects.

When the fear reaction occurs, the experience that arises could be called the *fear body*. From the present-moment perspective of mindfulness, you could say, "the fear body is present now."

The fear body is not easy to ignore. When it is present, the mind gets more excited and exchanges more and more information with the body. Body sensations intensify. Alarming thoughts appear and become louder. Your inner life goes on emergency mode.

The feelings of fear and anxiety seem to feed on the experience unfolding in the body and in the mind. The effect is like throwing gasoline on a fire. Panic and anxiety ignite. The feelings of panic and anxiety rage intensely in the body. The fear body feels more and more solid. As this happens, the proliferation of thoughts and worries fills the mind. And so it goes, on and on.

This is the vicious cycle in which people with panic disorder often become caught. Interrupting this cycle wherein bodily sensation leads to fearful thinking, which leads to more bodily sensation is difficult, but necessary in order to manage fear, anxiety, or panic.

But you don't have to have panic disorder to feel your fear body or to recognize when it has arrived. Whatever the cause of the fear body, your experience from the inside is *felt* and direct. While it is here, you are living in the fear body.

The fear body demands attention. The fear body experience is so strong that the mind can become absorbed in reactions to the body. So the real question is how to work with something so intense and demanding as the fear body.

The answer to that question brings us again to a paradox of mindfulness: the best results come when you let go of attachment to any desired outcome and allow yourself to experience things just as they are.

To practice mindfulness, you must be aware of, and establish and maintain contact with, the object of mindfulness. If you want mindfulness to help you manage the alarm and discomfort of the fear body, it is crucial that you learn to recognize and maintain awareness and contact with your body *just as it is* in each moment.

Doing this means allowing the experience of the body directly and accepting that experience just as it is. It is best to make this a way of approaching life in your body. *Mindfulness of the body,* we could call it. *Inhabiting your body with awareness* is another way to put it.

When your body is your object of mindfulness, your meditation practice becomes attention and awareness of the body in different situations—indeed, in all situations. You are there for sitting, walking, standing, and lying down. As you are able to be more present with the body experience anytime and in any position, then, when the fear body does arise, you will have developed the concentration and flexibility of attention required to manage what is unfolding.

Increasing Your Awareness of Your Body

Have you ever stopped to consider how rarely you pay attention to your body when the fear body, or other physical discomfort, is *not* present? How much of your life do you live above your nose? How much time, attention, and energy do you spend on mental activity such as thinking, planning, or remembering?

People seem to pay little attention below the nose except when the body yells for something to eat, has to void, wants sex, feels pain, or has some other immediate desire. Even then, in the midst of satisfying the immediate craving, their attention often moves back above the nose.

This habit of living above the nose, or out of the body, is common. In fact, people will go to considerable effort to keep their attention above the nose. Just look at any gym or health club. Have you ever noticed how many people are reading or listening to headsets while their body works out? Is their attention below the nose? Or is it in the future, the past, or a daydream?

Of course, people tune out of the body for many reasons. The reasons vary from the fact of being overloaded with work and trying to multitask, to not understanding the benefits of presence, to a deeper discomfort and ill ease with the body. At times, there can even be a disturbing sense of alienation from the body.

This alienation from the body requires attention and healing. In some cases, the alienation is so deep and the wounds causing it are so painful that good counseling is needed along with mindfulness. In other cases, the habits of inattention, absence, and disconnection from the body can be corrected with mindfulness practice only. In either case, teaching yourself to pay attention mindfully to your body is a great boost to the process of healing and transformation.

In this chapter you will learn a meditation practice called the body scan. You will also learn to do walking meditation. There are other mindfulness-oriented movement disciplines, such as yoga, tai chi, and chi kung. It is beyond the scope of this book to provide detailed instruction in these other practices, but there are many excellent books and videotapes available. Yoga classes are available in many urban and suburban areas.

Many people find that doing a mindful body practice enables them to feel their body as they have never felt it before. They are able to inhabit their bodies freshly and deeply. This leads to a positive experience of being in their bodies and with their bodies. Sadly, many people have not had such a deeply positive experience in or with their bodies since childhood, if at all.

 ## meditation practice: the body scan

In the body scan, you focus kind and allowing, nonjudging and nonstriving attention on the body itself. Attention is concentrated on each part of the body as closely and in as much detail as possible. You move your attention systematically throughout the body, excluding no part or region. Your focus is supported by linking breath awareness to the sensations in each region of the body. You practice allowing yourself to feel your body deeply, *from the inside*, as you breathe in and out of each region.

Paying mindful attention to the body leads to a deeper sense of connection with and awareness of the body. You have the experience of inhabiting your own body with a deeper and steadier sense of calm and relaxed attention. Your ability to focus and remain present on any part becomes much greater. And your body itself can relax deeply. All of these benefits establish a strong foundation for relating to and managing the fear body mindfully whenever it arises.

guided meditation:
body scan meditation

1. Take a position seated comfortably or lying down with pillows supporting your head and knees. Many people prefer to do the body scan lying down, and it works well as long as you remember that this is an exercise in *waking up*, not in falling asleep! Make sure you are warm enough. Allow enough time to do the practice slowly, at least thirty minutes, and practice going even more slowly as you become familiar with the meditation. When you are ready, let your eyes close.

2. Once settled in, spend a few moments recalling the key attitudes that form the foundation for mindfulness practice. Recall especially nonstriving, nonjudging, and acceptance. They are crucial to discovering how your body is right now, in this moment.

3. Let yourself feel the breath moving in and out of the body. Allow yourself to relax and feel the whole body. Feel the mass of it. Feel the points of contact and support with the chair or floor. Don't try to change anything you feel, just let it be. You are here for the *felt* experience of the body, just as it is. The practice is to experience the body, not to think about the body.

4. Bring attention to the toes on your left foot. Feel what you can. After a bit, try to direct your breathing in and out of the toes. Let this be a *sensation* you feel of the breath extending through the body to and from the toes. Don't make it a picture in your mind. Simply relax and see how much of the unfolding sensations of the breath and the toes you can connect with. Try to allow the breath sensation flowing in and out of the toes to sharpen your focus on what you are feeling in your toes. It is as if you become more present and more sharply focused on the toe sensations by holding them in the cradle of the breath.

5. If you don't feel any sensations, just notice that. Allow yourself to feel "no feeling." Notice if your mind makes up a story about this, and let the story go. Come back to the region of the toes.

6. Allow yourself to feel changes in sensation in the region of the toes. Feel the temperature, the contact with socks or shoes or air. Sharpen your attention as much as you can. Feel sensation in as much detail as you can, toe by toe, if you can. Stay with direct experience and with the breath sensations, in and out. Allow the sensations to come and go. Allow them to release naturally.

7. When you are ready to move on, take a deeper breath and release the focus on the toes. Keep attention on the breath sensation for a few breaths, then repeat steps 4, 5, and 6 focusing on the bottom of the foot. Then move to the heel, the top of the foot, and the ankle. Keep working with the breath and the body sensations this way. Continue to extend the breath awareness into and out of each region as you breathe in and out with the body sensations you discover there. Hold the sensations of each region in the cradle of the breath. The body sensations are the primary object of attention, while breathing in and out with them helps you stay connected and present.

8. Move through the regions of the left leg to the hip joint the same way. Continue holding the sensations in each region—lower leg, knee, upper leg—in focus as you breathe in and out. Then release the sensations in each region, staying present with the breath and moving on to the next region. Whenever your attention wanders, be patient with yourself and gently return awareness to the region you are focusing on and to the breath sensations.

9. In this way, continue to move slowly through the rest of your body. Scan the right foot and leg, the pelvis, the abdomen and lower back. Scan the chest and upper back. Go on to the shoulders. Scan the fingers, hands, and arms—first one side, then the other—and return to the shoulders. Maintain the focus on sensations and the breath as you move attention from region to region. Continue on through

the neck, the head, and all the regions of the face, including the inside of the mouth and throat.

10. When you have scanned all the regions of your body, allow yourself to rest with the breath and the body as they are. Let the breath sensations come in through the top of the head, as if you had a large opening there, and then wash through the entire body and exit through the toes of both feet simultaneously. Stay with this direction—in through head, through body, out through toes—as long as you like, then try reversing the direction. Breathe in through the toes, move breath through the body, and exit through the top of the head. Do this as long as you like.

11. By the time you have done all of this, you may not even feel your body. Don't worry about that. Simply allow yourself to rest in the silence and stillness that are present. Recognize the deep peace and ease that is possible in the body experience. Realize how much control and authority does lie within you.

12. When you are ready to stop your practice, simply acknowledge that, take a few deeper breaths, open the eyes, and begin to move the body slowly.

Practice the body scan daily, especially in the early days of building your mindfulness practice. You can also practice on specific regions without scanning the entire body. Try going into greater and greater detail with a particular region, moving inch by inch or millimeter by millimeter, over the face or the lower back, for example. Make it your own practice. Become comfortable and confident about connecting with your body.

meditation practice: mindful walking

The activity of walking offers an excellent opportunity to come into the present moment. Mindful walking means walking with primary attention focused on the activity of walking itself. In this way, the sensations and experience of walking link the mind, body, and present moment, just as the breath awareness practice does. In addition, by walking mindfully, you will begin to inhabit your moving body more consciously.

Mindful walking can be done as a formal meditation practice or informally as a way to connect to the present moment in the midst of physical activity and movement. The same principles of mindful walking can apply to mindful exercise or other moving activities.

guided meditation:
mindful walking

1. Find a place where you can walk back and forth for about fifteen to twenty paces without interruption and without feeling self-conscious. Plan to go back and forth on this meditation path for the time you do this formal period of walking meditation.

2. Stand at one end of your path and concentrate attention in your body. Notice the sensations that are present. Do something comfortable with your arms: either fold them in front or behind you, or let them hang loosely at your sides. Gather your attention in your feet, feeling the sensations there.

3. Slowly begin to lift one foot and begin walking. It helps to walk quite slowly, especially at first. Let your attention be on the unfolding sensations in your feet and legs as you walk. Bring attention in fine detail to the lifting of the foot, the stepping forward, and the placing of the foot on the ground. Notice how the weight shifts from foot to foot as you walk. Notice how the legs feel, and what movement in the body feels like. When attention moves away, or the mind wanders, gently return it to the sensations in the feet and legs.

4. Walk to the end of your path in this manner. Stop when you get there.

5. Bring attention to the experience of being stopped. Listen carefully to your body. Notice when the urge to move arises again, or the intention to turn and to resume walking. Become mindful of the arising of intention—it precedes all voluntary movement in the body. When you are ready, turn around and pause. Connect with the body and the sensations in your feet. Notice how it happens that you take the first step forward, and what that feels like.

6. Practice walking meditation this way at least fifteen to twenty minutes if you can. Notice whatever arises. If thoughts or sounds or anything else become very distracting, stop walking and focus attention on that. Remain mindful, noticing the distraction, then gently return focus to the feet and resume walking.

7. Although you begin walking at a very slow pace, you can experiment with different speeds, up to and beyond normal walking speed as you become more practiced. If you are very upset or agitated, it is often helpful to begin walking at a faster rate and then slow down as you become more concentrated and present. When walking fast, it may be easier to focus on a single sensation, such as the right foot pushing off or the left foot striking the ground. Let this single sensation become your object of attention, using it to anchor attention in the midst of rapid movement.

When walking "to get somewhere," as often as you can, practice walking mindfully. You can do this while walking at any speed. As in doing fast walking meditation, it may be helpful to focus on a single walking sensation as your anchor. Let the foot lifting or the foot striking the ground become your object of mindfulness, linking you to the present moment. Bring mindfulness into everyday activity this way. Enjoy how it can lead to a deeper connection with life. Walk mindfully in nature, in woods, or by the sea. Walk mindfully in times of urgency and hurry. Walk mindfully when you feel fear or anxiety, and discover the power you have to be present.

Keep in Mind

In this chapter we have looked more deeply into the intensity and demands of the fear body. The way to manage this intensity with mindfulness is to make mindfulness of the body a habit. The body scan and mindful walking are two ways to establish mindfulness of the body in daily life. As you make conscious bodily experience a daily practice, the fear body becomes just another way the body can be. By breathing and remaining mindful of it, you gain freedom from its distortions and limitations on your life.

chapter 11

bringing full attention to life

Acentral truth emerges in profound ways as you practice being present: you are not your thoughts, feelings, or sensations. No matter how intense, pleasant, or unpleasant the thought, feeling, or sensation might be, it can be observed using the mirror of mindfulness and can be seen to be changing and impermanent. This is a crucial fact to remember when you are trying to free yourself from the bonds of fear, panic, or anxiety.

Hijacked by Desire and Ill Will

There is intense unpleasantness in the fear reaction and its extreme form, the panic attack. Everything in you screams to get away from it. There is a deep and disturbing feeling of vulnerability and exposure. All of your physical and psychological systems are mobilized to fight or to flee. But what can you do if there is nothing to fight except the unpleasant feeling itself—as in anxiety and panic? Where can you go to get away when the unpleasant feeling is inside your own skin? What can you do when the feelings are so intense that they defeat your every effort, even those aimed at concentrating attention on the breath or a body sensation?

As human beings, we all have developed deep and habitual reactions to moment-by-moment experience. These reactions are driven directly by the feeling of pleasantness, unpleasantness, or neutrality associated with the experience in the moment. The reactions to this moment-by-moment feeling of pleasantness, unpleasantness, or neutrality are expressed in psychological and physical ways. The reactions themselves are simple. The tendency is to grasp or hold onto the pleasant, reject or push away the unpleasant, and "space out" or disconnect if there is no strong feeling quality (the situation feels neutral).

For the most part, these reactions occur rapidly and out of awareness. You usually do not realize how much energy you spend trying to hang on to the pleasant feeling or trying to avoid the unpleasant one. Your energy is hijacked by desire for the pleasant, or ill will for the unpleasant. What you probably do notice is the experience of frustration, struggle, fear, or anxiety. In turn, these experiences become another set of unpleasant feelings to avoid or push away.

The tendency toward grasping or avoiding experiences has important implications. For example, when fear, panic, or anxiety arises in all of its unpleasantness in the present moment, it is very likely that you find yourself in a familiar pattern of thoughts, feelings, and actions aimed at ridding yourself of the experience almost immediately. This reaction is driven by aversion or ill will toward what is here in this moment, and results in a desperate sense of needing to "fix" the problem or to "do something" immediately. This habitual reaction then unfolds in cognitive, emotional, and physical dimensions. The unpleasantness of the reaction feeds the feeling of needing to escape.

Allen's Story

Five years ago, when he was forty-seven, Allen suffered a mild heart attack. Although he recovered well, Allen developed a strong fear that he would die from another heart attack. After a time, he began to have panic attacks.

Since then, Allen has seen different doctors and therapists who have suggested various treatments for his panic attacks. In addition to using medication, Allen has been taught biofeedback and visual imagery. He has had some counseling. He has been in support groups. He has had some benefits from all of these, but admits there are still times when the panic returns and is stronger than his ability to manage it with the therapies he has learned.

Allen has come to feel that the panic attacks are his enemy and that the panic is often stronger than he is. The more he reflects on this me-versus-my-panic relationship, the more depressed and hopeless he becomes. When there is a sensation of panic, Allen's next experience is often a sense of dread and fear about what that means. Allen has become a prisoner to fear and worry about his panic, as well as to the panic itself.

Allen has come to the place where he meets the unpleasantness of his panic attacks with intense aversion. He greatly wants to be rid of all of it. The sensations lead to thoughts and more sensations, all of which are unpleasant. Allen describes one of the low points:

> *I wake in the middle of the night shaky, sweating, and afraid. Immediately I know there will be no more sleep this night and feel angry, hopeless, and depressed. I get up and sit in a comfortable chair. I try to do the visualization, then the relaxation exercises. I barely get started when the panic really gets going and distracts me. I try again, but can't keep my mind on it. I feel very upset now, even agitated. I try listening to some relaxing*

music, but the panic won't go away and I find myself feeling worse and worse. I start to get mad at myself. I start to curse kind of quietly to myself. I hate it when that happens, and I start to hate myself for not being able to handle it better. Everything seems to get worse. I sweat, my heart pounds, my mind races with scary thoughts about dying. At a time like this, I actually start to think about suicide. Maybe I ought to go ahead and die on my own terms. Sometimes I even begin to make a plan. Then I get hold of myself and remember my wife and kids, and it helps me let go of the suicide thoughts. I wouldn't do it, really. But I just get so desperate because I can't seem to do anything in those bad times that helps.

Staying Present with What Is Unpleasant

Can you relate to Allen's struggle? When you see the elements of your life experience as the enemy because they're unpleasant, suffering and powerlessness are almost unavoidable.

The painful and upsetting things never seem to leave as quickly as one would like. What can be done with these stubborn and unpleasant visitors?

Whether it is fear, panic, anxiety, physical pain, illness, or loss, there will always be something that comes along that you cannot completely cure, push away, or escape. This is where mindfulness can help.

Instead of fighting or trying to flee from the unpleasantness, mindfulness invites you to turn toward experience. Staying present with calm and relaxed attention, you are encouraged to investigate and connect with the experience. Freedom from suffering in the unpleasant experience comes from learning to soften and relax, and remain present and aware in the midst of it. This calls for making room inside for the experience and allowing it to unfold within the space you open.

There is relief in the next mindful breath you take. Even one breath taken mindfully can change your relationship to the contents of your life experience in this moment. The breath can help you open to your inner capacity for spaciousness. As well as gaining immediate benefit from the change in relationship to what is here, by remaining present and seeing clearly, you have your best chance to discover any additional responses that might improve the situation.

So far, you have been practicing mindfulness with a focus on the breath sensations and on the body experience. These meditation practices have emphasized concentrating attention narrowly and discovering how mindfulness can connect you deeply with the object of attention as you hold it in focus.

When attention wanders, the practice has been to return it gently to the breath or body sensations. When there are distractions, or simply as a way of focusing attention more sharply, you have also practiced breathing into and out of any intense distraction or body region. In this way, you have been using the actual sensations of the in and out breath to help you stay connected with the focus of your meditation and with the present moment. This helps you stay connected and work with powerful mental states like fear, anxiety, and panic.

At this point, it is time to take a wider view in your mindfulness practice. In essence, you are now invited to make whatever experience is most dominant or most insistent the object of mindfulness. Nothing is excluded from your kind and allowing attention. In this approach, there are no "distractions." Whatever arises becomes the object of mindfulness. Your practice leads you to intimacy with each experience, each "distraction," via attention and awareness.

From this expanded perspective, life in each moment becomes deeper and richer. The practice is literally to connect with increased sensitivity to whatever presents itself.

Opening through awareness, your recognition and understanding of habits of ill will and desire deepens. As this understanding grows, you will be able to stand firm in who you are and release the old habits of grasping or avoiding experience, and the suffering that brings.

Letting Go of Your Agenda

You might be asking yourself about now, "How can I stay present when the worry or the panic or the fear is so strong?" You may have had some real success in calming and relaxing the mind and body using breath awareness and body scanning, and you may not want to open to the "bad" feelings you are trying so hard to get away from. You may have been using the breath awareness or the body scan to make the anxiety or panic "go away," and may even have thought you did on some occasions.

If you can identify with any of these themes or variations on them, you might still be caught in the me-versus-my-problem mentality. And you are not alone! This is a very common situation, and you should know you have not done anything wrong or made any mistakes. But it is critical that you do not stay stuck in this mentality.

If you have been trying to "use the meditation" to "make the anxiety go away," just recognize that. It is an example of how truly powerful the habits of grasping and avoiding experience are.

Challenge yourself to look more deeply at your own experience so far. It is crucial to recognize when the urge to fix things or to change things is present. That urge must be made an object of mindfulness like everything else. Isn't now a good time to do it? Can you open to your desire to change how things are, to fix things, and simply allow that urge to be, making it the object of attention?

In all likelihood, when you have felt any benefit from your meditation, it was because you were including nonstriving, nonjudging, acceptance, and the rest of the key attitudes in your practice. When you felt frustrated and said, "It doesn't seem to work," most likely you had a goal or outcome you wanted and didn't feel it happening. You were likely striving for peace, relaxation, freedom from thoughts or worrying and so on, and judging yourself and the meditation and probably this book in the process.

Embracing the Entire Range of Experience

Remember that practicing mindfulness means exploring ways to be more aware and awake in *all* corners of your life. It calls for recognizing the entire range of inner experience and trusting yourself to connect with, and to allow, all of these experiences. It invites a compassionate connection with the contents of your inner life and a real willingness to allow and experience each one.

In this sense, practicing mindfulness becomes a process of growth and self-discovery supported by kindness and compassion for your own pain and distress. It is an art that you teach yourself. Give yourself permission to move at your own speed as you learn this art.

You are invited to discover a spaciousness within that can contain the flux of experience. You can learn to apply precise, noninterfering awareness and sensitivity to each element of life experience as it arises in the present moment. As you discover the spaciousness and stillness within, you will be able to listen for the song of each experience and to recognize the lesson it has for you.

meditation practice: choiceless awareness

Choiceless awareness is a practice of gently opening and kindly including whatever is here in your field of attention. This practice is also sometimes called *bare attention* or *mindfulness of the full field of awareness.* It emphasizes recognizing and resting with whatever is predominant in the field of awareness in the present moment.

The predominant thing changes after a bit and is replaced by something else. The practice is to stay relaxed and grounded in the present moment and to recognize and keep attention on whatever is here now. Doing this involves recognizing and accepting the elements in the changing flow of experience.

Practicing choiceless awareness means literally practicing a different relationship to the elements of life experience. Instead of the usual and habitual way of fighting with, fleeing from, or identifying with what is here, everything gets equal attention. Everything gets noticed by kind awareness. The method is the spaciousness and steadiness of mindful attention.

In this practice, *bare* means nonjudging, noninterfering, and allowing. *Attention* means mindfulness, wakefulness to what is here, awareness. *Choiceless* means literally that: making no choice. Allowing whatever is in the foreground to be the object of attention. You do not leave what is here, but look more deeply, listen more fully, feel more completely, as you stay present with it.

The instruction is simple. Establish attention in the present moment and open awareness to what is here. Then stay in the present moment, holding the changing experiences in mindfulness as they unfold and releasing them as they disappear.

Through this practice, your ability to work with the intensity of fear, panic, and anxiety will increase. These experiences will be held more easily in the spaciousness of mindful attention. Their tendency to intrude and drive you will diminish. You can regain control of your life.

The following guided meditation is divided into four parts. The first part is a preliminary activity to remind you about setting up the conditions for formal practice. The second part is a reminder to establish mindfulness on the breath, as you have already learned to do. The third part is a detailed instruction in opening awareness to the different senses and the experiences at each sense gate. The fourth part is a detailed guided meditation for choiceless awareness.

The methods in the first three parts of this exercise provide a foundation. Parts 2 and 3 can be practiced as separate meditations themselves. The actual practice of choiceless awareness is to be aware, to not hold on to anything or try to make anything happen, and to simply open awareness to all that comes and goes.

It may take some time and practice for your concentration and mindfulness to become strong enough so that you are not swept away or lost in the river of experience flowing through the senses in each moment. Grounding yourself in the foundation practices and being patient will provide the support you need, however, and soon you will become more comfortable with the choiceless awareness practice itself.

guided meditation:
choiceless awareness

Part 1: Establishing the Conditions and Attitudes for Meditation

1. Take your seat in a comfortable position in the place you choose for formal meditation. Make sure you have allowed enough time for practice (twenty to thirty minutes at least) and that you have minimized the risk of distractions and interruptions.

2. Spend the first few moments of your practice period remembering and reflecting on the key attitudes that form the foundation for mindfulness practice. Mindfulness is about noninterfering, allowing presence. Recall nonjudging, patience, beginner's mind, trust, nonstriving, acceptance, and letting go. Each of these will be needed at some time or another as you practice and deepen mindfulness. Pay particular attention to any reactions you are having to what you are doing. Try to let them go. Let go of any agenda for

changing things. Acceptance is the willingness to see things just as they are and to let them be.

Part 2: Establishing Attention on the Breath in the Present Moment

3. Practice awareness of breathing as you have learned to do. Gather and collect awareness on the sensations of the breath and the heaviness and presence of the body. Allow the belly to remain soft and relaxed. Use the technique of quietly noting or naming "in," "out," "space," "touch," and so on if it helps you sharpen your attention on breath and body. Do this long enough to feel grounded and present. Keep the focus more narrow at first, centered on breath sensation and body presence. Allow yourself to relax into what is happening. Try to feel the space around the breath sensations and the body feelings.

Part 3: Establishing Mindfulness of All Sense Experience

4. After you have established calm and focused attention through connection with breath and body, widen the focus to include any and all sounds that may be present. Allow yourself to hear as carefully as you can. If you find yourself commenting or reacting to a sound, notice that and let it go. Come back to the activity of listening directly. Allow yourself to hear the sound without commentary. Just the sound as it is. Try to notice the sound vibration as intense or soft, low or midrange or high, near or far. Listen deeply for the space between the sounds. Notice when the vibration arises, how it changes, and how it fades. If it helps to focus attention, you could note quietly, "hearing, hearing" with each sound. Try not to get stuck in thoughts about the sound. Recognize thoughts such as "that is a loud car" or "there goes my telephone again." These are just thoughts that have taken you away from the direct experience of hearing the sound. They will happen. Praise yourself when you realize you are not simply listening and go back to that. Try to rest in the spaciousness of mindful

listening. Allow the sense of spaciousness to include and hold all the sounds, and the silence itself.

5. Whenever you get lost, confused, agitated, or distracted, relax. Gently take the narrow focus on the breath again. Reestablish mindfulness on the breath. Practice awareness of breathing for a few breaths. Let the breath be your anchor in the present moment. You can always come back to the breath sensation. If the distraction is intense, let it be and try breathing in and out with it until it changes or until you can feel the breath more clearly. Notice your abdomen. Let it soften and relax. Come back to the breath and the soft belly as often as you need to in order to stay present and grounded in the now.

6. Keep your body and belly soft and relaxed as much as possible. When you are ready, widen the focus to include all the changing body sensations as well as the breath and sounds. Let yourself experience the inner body, the felt sense of your body. Keep it simple. Let go of trying to make anything happen. You do not have to go looking for breath, sensation, or sound. Simply let them come into your awareness. Relax and soften into the body and keep the awareness open and inviting. Notice the body sensations as vibrations, pressure, contractions, expansions, warmth, coolness, and so on. Notice how they come and go, moment by moment. Again, if it helps you to focus, use a quiet mental notation to help you connect with each thing that is happening. You might say, "tingling," "pressure," "pulsing," "contracting and hardening," "softening and releasing," and so on, for the flow of sensations. Try to soften and allow each sensation to be, in the open space of awareness.

7. Open the awareness again and include any smells and tastes that are present. You do not have to manufacture these. Simply rest in awareness and notice what might be present. Be alert for the reactions and judgments of thinking about any smell or taste. Allow yourself the direct experience. Is it sweet? Sour? Salty? Stuffy? Heavy? Light? Where is it sensed: in the nose, or the mouth? Does it change, move, get stronger or weaker?

8. Allow yourself to relax. Don't try too hard. Practice being soft, open, and receptive. Stay grounded in the sensations of the breath and the body. Allow yourself to experience directly the breath, the body sensations, the sounds, the smells, and the tastes. If you are using a quiet mental notation or labeling of experience to help stay connected, the noting should be only a whisper in your mind. Let at least 95 percent of your attention be on the direct experience of feeling, hearing, smelling, or tasting. Whenever you are lost or agitated or distracted for any reason, return to the breath awareness. Establish attention on the breath. Relax. Breathe in and out with whatever is happening. Keep the belly soft. Then open to the spacious awareness that includes everything.

9. Open the awareness to include all forms of thinking. There are many of them. Just acknowledge what is going on now. Is there commentary? Judgment? Planning? Remembering? Storytelling? What is the difference between being lost in a story and recognizing that storytelling is going on? That is a moment of mindfulness. Notice certain themes in your thinking. Is it the Love story? The Boss story? The Anxiety story? The Worry about Whatever story? Learning to become aware of these stories is a moment of mindfulness. In this practice the relative truth or importance of the thoughts is not the issue. All thoughts are treated the same. Allow them to be as they are instead of meeting them with more thoughts, stories, or explanations. They are just thoughts. They are just something here in this moment along with the breath, sensations, sounds, and everything else. Find the spaciousness within and allow any thoughts to float there. Rest in the open space of nonjudging, nonthinking, allowing awareness.

Part 4: Practicing Choiceless Awareness

10. Include everything that arises in your practice of choiceless awareness. Whatever it is, it is just another condition that is here now. Recognize mind-states and emotions like anger, fear, boredom, sleepiness, restlessness, desire for something else, impatience, calm, peace,

excitement, joy, jealousy, rage, kindness, love, and com-passion. Allow yourself to open to the entire range of your experience. Feel the energy associated with each condi-tion or emotion. Practice holding each one in the open space of awareness without identifying with it, grasping at it, or pushing it away.

11. Open to everything that is present. Each sound, each sen-sation, each smell, each taste, each thought, each emotion is treated the same way. Each is just another object aris-ing in awareness now. Notice the one that is in the fore-ground now. Relax into softness and allow that object to be here. Pay attention and connect with it as deeply as you can. Let yourself feel as much spaciousness as possi-ble and rest there as you pay attention to each object that comes forward. Try to stay connected. Hold it in view as long as it is here. You might need to note it several times before it changes and is replaced by another object. For example, you might note, "hearing, hearing, hearing," or "pressure, pressure, pressure," or "thinking about work, thinking about work, thinking about work." If the noting is distracting, just let it go and stay 100 percent with the direct sensation of each object. Be patient and stay present.

12. Continue your practice this way. This is the practice of choiceless awareness. You are strengthening awareness and presence. Remember to keep the belly soft. Relax. Allow things to present themselves. When fear or worry or even panicky feelings arise, try to meet them with the same kind attention. Look deeply. Feel deeply. Listen deeply. Allow them to come and go. Breathe with them consciously if it helps you to maintain the connection. When they stay, pay careful attention to what is happen-ing in your mind and body. Shine the light of mindfulness directly on whatever is the strongest or loudest part of the fear, panic, or anxiety. Hold that part in mindful aware-ness. Return attention to the breath and soft belly if nec-essary. Breathe consciously. Then allow the thoughts to go on. Notice their "attitude" or "tone of voice." Feel the body sensations. Allow the softening and relaxing

wherever possible. Remember patience and trust. Notice thoughts about failing and feelings of hopelessness and despair. Have kindness and compassion for yourself. See the thoughts as just thoughts. Feel the feelings in the body and notice how they come, change, and go. Keep the wider view. Rest in spacious and open awareness of all that comes and goes. Allow yourself to sense each object, but do not remain identified with it or swept away by it.

13. End your practice by opening your eyes and moving gently.

Suggestions for Practicing Choiceless Awareness

As you learn to do this practice formally, you will also be able to carry it over informally into daily life. You will learn to find and to rest in the open space of awareness more often throughout the day.

Formal Meditation Practice

Practice for at least twenty minutes at a time when doing choiceless awareness as your formal meditation. Over time, you can move up to sessions of thirty, forty-five, or even sixty minutes. Similar to what happens in an exercise program, you are building a level of "fitness" or strength to meditate, and it is important that you practice long enough to get stronger.

Expect to meet resistance. Your mind doesn't want to be trained. There will be doubt, boredom, irritation, desire for other things, restlessness, and sleepiness. Please notice your reaction to any of these or anything else. Make the reaction or the resistance the object of mindfulness just like anything else. Just keep practicing being present as best you can. Recognizing and staying present with whatever resistance you feel builds real power and gives you freedom from the unconscious patterns of reactivity that drive daily life.

As you gain experience with practicing choiceless awareness, begin to let go of the written instructions or the tape or CD you have made. Trust yourself to be able to establish attention in the breath and body and to open to whatever is here. As you practice over time, your ability to refine attention, sharpen focus, and hold the predominant object in view will strengthen. Be patient with yourself. Don't try to get anywhere or make anything different. Just practice letting things be the way they are and knowing something about how that is by paying attention on purpose.

Informal Meditation Practice

Try practicing choiceless awareness informally in the different situations of your daily life. Allow yourself to hear the sounds, taste the tastes, smell the smells, all directly and without commentary or judgment. When you notice the thinking in any form, note and welcome it. Try to remain friendly and open to all that you notice. Your thoughts are *not* the enemy. Thinking is just another condition. Use it when it is useful. Notice it when it is not useful. Just thinking.

Look for opportunities to take a time-out from *doing*. Allow yourself to *be* with what is here. Really see the beautiful sunset. Really taste the delicious food. Really feel the hand of your loved one in yours. Open more fully to the richness of your life by strengthening presence.

When fear, panic, or anxiety arise, notice your reactions to the unpleasantness. Try to find compassion and kindness for yourself and the pain you feel in the moment. Keep it simple. As best you can, see and feel what is happening as deeply as you can, with attention and nonjudging awareness. Can you notice the changing patterns of thought and sensation in mind and body?

After you have met fear, panic, and anxiety with calm and kind awareness, ask what needs to be done. If there is a specific step or action you need to take, do it. In this way, your actions are guided by presence. Being informs doing.

Keep in Mind

You are not your thoughts, feelings, or sensations. These are events in the present moment that can be observed kindly and compassionately in the mirror of mindfulness. Learning to experience these events mindfully through the practice of choiceless awareness will give you new power to live with fear, panic, and anxiety.

These events include especially what is happening in your inner life. As you learn to recognize and witness the changes in these inner experiences, you also discover your deepest quality of being and the peace and stability within you.

chapter 12

befriending your anxious mind

Larry Rosenberg, a well-respected meditation teacher, once observed that mindfulness without kindness is not mindfulness. What does this mean?

So far, we have understood and practiced mindfulness as allowing, nonjudging awareness. A crucial element embedded in this allowing is the spirit of friendliness, or kindness. Kindness here means a welcoming, friendly, and generous attitude. Having this attitude toward whatever arises as you are practicing mindfulness is essential.

Kindness as an inner quality is something that you can actually practice.

You already have the capacity for kindness in you. You do not have to manufacture it. You do, however, have to cultivate it. Cultivating kindness means learning to recognize and overcome the obstacles that block your awareness of your deep capacity to be kind.

Cultivating Kindness

You can practice kindness in your actions. The quality of kindness shines through when you do something for someone or respond kindly in a situation.

Perhaps you have seen the popular bumper sticker that advises practicing random acts of kindness. This idea encourages acting kindly without expecting anything in return. Kindness is freely given. Undoubtedly, you have already done kind acts for others many times in your life. But there is more to kindness than external action.

There is an interior feeling of kindness behind all kind actions. This feeling can be strengthened through meditation practice. The kindness you feel is directly related to your sense of well-being and connection with life and others. It is an essential feeling of well-wishing. It has warmth and is friendly. This kindness reflects the capacity to love.

Meditation teacher Jack Kornfield (1993) speaks to this relationship between happiness and love: "The longing for love and the movement of love is underneath all of our activities. The happiness we discover in life is not about possessing or owning or even understanding. Instead, it is the discovery of this capacity to love, to have a loving, free, and wise relationship with all of life. (p. 18)"

Cultivating Compassion

Kindness supports the presence and growth of compassion as well. There is a deep link between kindness and compassion. In our common experience as human beings, we all share the feelings of warmth and kindness, and we all feel the inevitable pains of living, aging, and dying.

Compassion can be understood as a powerful inner feeling that involves the opening of one's own heart in sympathy and tenderness in the presence of pain or sorrow in another. Along with this opening, there is a sense of connection with the other. And often there is a strong urge to take action to relieve the pain.

While people may be deeply moved by the presence of pain in others, all too often they have little or no compassion for the pain and sorrow they feel in themselves. They view their own pain as vulnerability, or consider their own sorrow to be a sign of weakness. Anxious or fearful people who judge their own anxiety as a defect or failure are especially likely to deny themselves compassion.

As we have seen, the negative self-talk and critical attitudes that often grow around experiences of fear, anxiety, and panic can be the worst stressors that are present. To break this toxic cycle of meanness and criticism means developing the capacity to feel compassion for your own pain and suffering.

The Power of Kindness and Compassion

We saw in chapter 4 how thoughts and attitudes are very powerful, and how they have the "connections" through brain and body links to exert their influence on the body's fear system. Working through the mind-body connection, such habits of mean thinking can be strikingly deep and strong. Consider the destructive potential of self-critical thoughts like Ellen's.

Ellen's Story

Ellen was in her late fifties when she enrolled in a mindfulness-based meditation class. She joined the class to get help with her experiences of intense anxiety and panic attacks, disturbed and nonrestful sleep, and chronic pain.

Ellen had been married to an abusive, alcoholic man for many years. She finally divorced him, and a few months later came to the class.

One day after several weeks in the course, during which she had practiced mindfulness faithfully, Ellen arrived late to class. She was visibly upset and explained what had happened.

"I had a flat tire on my car," she told the class, "and it was very stressful."

Someone asked Ellen what it had been like.

She paused for a moment before she answered. Then with an angry and anxious tone she said, "I kept telling myself how stupid I was to have a flat tire. Stupid! Stupid! I told myself, 'You are too stupid to live.' I say that to myself a lot. Whenever something goes wrong. *You are too stupid to live.* My husband used to say that to me a lot. Now I say it to myself."

Are You Practicing Meanness?

Since kindness can be practiced, it is also important to understand that its opposite attitude, meanness, can also be practiced. In fact, meanness is practiced quite a lot. Most often, we aim it at ourselves. We usually don't fully recognize how mean we are to ourselves. This meanness is a habit of thinking and feeling that arises often and is felt deeply in the body.

Meanness expresses itself in critical tones and self-statements. You might tell yourself, "I am such a jerk," or "I am so stupid," or "I always make a mess of things."

The inner habit of mean thoughts and comments, and the related sensations of hardening and contraction in the body, arise repeatedly. It may seem that you have always had them. Until you actually bring attention to them, you may not even know where they are. Most of the time, you probably do not even notice them, at least not until the feelings or the comments are especially uncomfortable or harsh.

Like Ellen, you can be living in a world of inner meanness and come to identify it as self. You can come to believe all the harsh judgments, and live in the fear body whenever the judges speak.

When this meanness happens in you, you become your own worst stressor. No matter how bad the situation is, your mean attitude amplifies and adds to your misery, usually through the addition of criticism, judgment, and blame.

Of course, meanness also lashes out at others. "You," "they," "that one"—all become the objects of the criticism. The tone of anger and hostility that drives the meanness spares no one.

By practicing mindfulness, kindness, and compassion in a steady and committed way, you will begin to recognize the habits of meanness toward self or another when they surface. You can become free of their hold. Their reach into your other experiences and relationships will diminish. The toxic effects of meanness in your body will be reduced.

The way to manage the damaging energies of anger and hostility lies in establishing a conscious connection with them in the present moment. This means establishing a kind attention on your inner experience of anger and hostility, recognizing it as experience, not as self. It means being a friend to yourself and to the anger.

The same applies to fear and anxiety. Indeed, fear and anxiety usually lie beneath anger and hostility. Can you learn to befriend your anxiety and fear when they arise? Can you hold them in kind awareness?

It is only when you can stay connected with the present moment that real caring can arise. The kindness within can shine through, and compassion can awaken. To evoke this kindness, you must teach yourself to stay present with pain and difficulty as well as everything else.

Opening to the Pain in and around You

Have you ever stopped to ask the question: What is my relationship to the pain I feel? This includes the pain of fear and the pain of anxiety and panic.

You *do* have a relationship, you just may not recognize it. For many people, the relationship they have with any kind of pain is one of denial and dismissal. For others, the relationship is flavored by anger, fear, or a desperate attempt to escape the pain. Driven by pain, people fall into patterns of addiction and despair.

Remember Pema Chodron's story of the old woman telling her, "Don't go letting life harden your heart"? Has your relationship to pain caused your heart to harden? Are you less connected with life as a result? Do you feel less alive?

To practice mindfulness means to pay attention to life with an open heart. Meditation can actually help this way. Meditation is a heart-opening activity!

On a meditation retreat once, I entered a phase when either sitting or walking, all of my periods of meditation were consumed by angry, destructive images and stories filled with hostility and rage. When I asked the teacher about this, he responded with great gentleness and kindness. He told me, "Beneath anger is fear. Beneath fear is a belief about something. Keep sitting with each thing and let it be. Let it reveal itself to you. When you get to the belief, investigate that. Is the belief true? Is the belief you?" Sitting with the experience, I connected with deep feelings of self-doubt and inadequacy about a new job situation. Sitting longer, I found that the feelings left me. I saw how untrue they actually were.

We all have a relationship with pain and habits for dealing with it. We all have developed attitudes and views about the pain we feel. In many cases we have also developed an identity around the pain. To the extent these attitudes and identity have become fixed, we are prisoners of the pain.

How might this be true for you? How does it apply to the impact of fear, anxiety, or panic in your life?

Practicing mindfulness wholeheartedly requires the willingness to pay attention, stay present, and investigate your deep inner pain—including the pain of fear, anxiety, or even panic. Approaching the pain with kindness and compassion is crucial. Meeting pain with anger does not help. Meeting fear or anxiety in oneself with anger or hostility simply multiplies it.

Meditation teacher Sharon Salzberg has been a leader in bringing Western students meditation practices focused on kindness and compassion. In her 1995 book *Loving-Kindness: The Revolutionary Art of Happiness,* Salzberg describes compassion meditation as "purifying and transforming our relationship to suffering, whether it is our own or that of others. Being able to acknowledge suffering, open to it, and respond to it with tenderness of heart allows us to join with all beings, and to realize that we are never alone. (p. 117)"

In this chapter, we will learn loving-kindness meditation, a practice aimed at strengthening attitudes of kindness and compassion. As you will see, it is a basic meditation practice that is friendly to any faith tradition.

Mindfulness helps you recognize any mean thoughts or feelings that are here. The meanness may be blocking you from experiencing your deep capacity for kindness and compassion. You can learn to hold the feelings of anger and meanness with more kindness. You can teach yourself to meet fear and anxiety with compassion. This is deep inner work that allows you to access a profoundly healing dimension in your being.

meditation practice: loving-kindness

With a kind and compassionate heart, all you attempt—including your practice of mindfulness—will flow more easily. Loving-kindness meditation uses repeated phrases, images, and feelings to evoke kindness and compassion. It is not exactly a mindfulness practice, yet the qualities it cultivates are crucial to the practice of mindfulness.

This meditation is not about sentimentality or about manufacturing "good" feelings. It is about connecting with and cultivating a capacity for kindness and friendliness that is already within you. At first it may feel mechanical or clumsy. It may arouse painful feelings like anger or grief. Don't let this disturb you. Keep up your practice and discover what happens next. When you have difficulty, hold yourself with kindness and compassion.

When you do loving-kindness meditation as a formal practice, begin with sessions of fifteen to twenty minutes and increase to thirty to forty-five minutes at your own pace.

guided meditation: loving-kindness meditation

1. Take a comfortable position, either seated or lying down.

2. Bring awareness to the breath and the body as they are in this moment.

3. Let your body relax and be at rest. As best you can, let your mind be quiet. Let go of plans and preoccupations.

4. Allow a feeling of kindness and friendliness to arise within. Recalling a loved one or a pet can help to nurture this feeling.

5. Begin by focusing kindness on yourself. It may help to find an image of yourself in your imagination or to say your own name quietly to yourself as you repeat the phrases below. Without kindness for yourself, it is almost impossible to be kind or compassionate with others. With the focus on yourself, begin to recite the following phrases:

   May I be happy.

   May I be healed and healthy.

   May I be filled with peace and ease.

   May I be safe.

6. Continue repeating the phrases. Let them be like a song you sing quietly to yourself. As you repeat them, adjust the language so that you find the exact words and phrases to best nourish kindness in your own heart. You might also try the following:

   May I be free from all pain and sorrow.

   May I be at ease and at peace.

   May I be free from fear, anxiety, and worry.

   May I be well.

7. Repeat the phrases that work best for you, over and over. Let the feelings penetrate and fill your body and mind. Experiment with other phrases if you need to. Use phrases that resonate deeply within.

8. When you feel ready, in the same meditation period or in a separate period, expand the focus of your kindness to include others. Move to someone who has cared for you, to someone who is a friend, to someone whom you have no strong feelings for or don't know well, to one who causes pain or hurt, and to all living things, including animals and plants. Experiment. Don't be afraid.

9. Practice as long as you like. When you are ready to stop, gently open the eyes and allow the body to stretch slowly.

Notice how you feel without judgment or commentary. Allow yourself to feel what you feel.

Suggestions for Practicing Loving-Kindness

With some practice a steady sense of kindness can develop. You will be able to work with directing kindness toward all kinds of people—even difficult people.

With time you can learn to practice loving-kindness anywhere. As you silently practice repeating the phrases of loving-kindness in grocery checkout lines, in doctors' waiting rooms, in traffic, in the middle of crowds, on the streets, or in a thousand other places, a deeper feeling of connection and compassion for all of life arises. A deeper sense of calm will fill your life and keep you connected to the present moment.

Keep in Mind

Mindfulness has a welcoming and friendly quality. To befriend what arises in awareness is essential to avoid the habits of meanness and judgment that lead to feelings of isolation and suffering. Befriending means meeting pain and distress, fear, anxiety, and even panic with kindness, compassion, and nondenying awareness. The qualities of kindness and compassion—toward yourself and others—can be cultivated by including loving-kindness meditation in your daily practice.

part 3

applying mindfulness to fear, anxiety, and panic

chapter 13

common
concerns
about these
meditation
practices

Now you have had a chance to do some meditation practice with mindfulness and kindness. It is likely that you have developed some questions based in your direct experience of these meditation practices. This is good. It shows that you have been practicing! You are gaining intimacy with your interior life through attention and awareness.

One of the central themes of this book is that you can better manage fear, anxiety, and panic if you can learn to make each of those unpleasant states the object of mindfulness.

You will be most successful if you make mindfulness a way of living. It should become an approach to life itself rather than a "technique" that you apply only when fear, anxiety, or panic is present. If you have gotten into daily habits of mindfulness and kindness, then when fear, anxiety, or panic arises, you will find it much easier to treat it as just something else to practice with. Establishing a daily meditation practice is the best way to make mindfulness a way of living.

As you practice meditation and mindfulness in a consistent and ongoing way, it is natural to develop questions. Asking *your* questions and finding appropriate responses to them will deepen your meditation practice. Questioning and practice together will also add strength and confidence as you meet and manage fear, anxiety, or panic, or any other stressors or challenges in life.

Reading other books, listening to tapes, and talking with other meditators and meditation teachers are all ways to answer questions that you might have. But remember, the best answers will always come from your own practice experience with mindfulness, in formal meditation and informally in daily life. Always test the answer from anyone else against your own experience. How does it work for you?

To cultivate a mindful life takes real practice and commitment. You need commitment, and the patience, acceptance, and determination that accompany it, to challenge the powerful habits of perception and strongly held attitudes that we, as human beings, develop over a lifetime.

Meditation teachers like to say that meditation is a training of the mind and heart. When you meditate consistently and with proper instructions and effort, you are training yourself to overcome the power of old habits. In particular, the habits of inattention, distraction, and absence, plus those of criticism and constant commentary, can be big obstacles and are important to overcome. This training of the mind and heart will also help you overcome habitual reactions to fear, anxiety, and panic.

When you learn to meditate, you train your mind in peaceful abiding. This means you are training your mind and heart and body to remain calm, at peace, and aware in the present moment.

Remember that you already have what it takes for peaceful abiding. From the perspective of mindfulness, you already have a mind and heart that are joyful, calm, and clear. No matter what you think is wrong with you, there is more that is right than wrong.

Unfortunately, you may not always agree. This is probably because you have encountered obstacles, both in life and in your meditation practice. These obstacles are created by habits and conditioning that block your sense of connection with—and full expression of—the deep and profound inner qualities of stillness and clarity.

It is important to see these obstacles for what they are. They are not you. They are not permanent. It is only by practicing meditation and the various mindfulness methods that you will become aware of the obstacles and limiting habits in your own life. From this point of view, any question you have is a good one. An interesting thing about these obstacles and habits is we all have them!

The questions and concerns you are about to read are ones that people have whenever they take up mindfulness meditation (or, indeed, many other types of meditation). They reflect the basic human experience of the wandering mind, desire for pleasant things, and aversion or anger toward unpleasant things. The commonness of these concerns shows that we are more alike than different as human beings.

Common Concerns about Meditation Practice

I don't have time to meditate. What should I do?

Have you made meditation a priority? Having a meditation practice is just like having any other commitment in your life. You have to make it a priority. It can help to remember your original motivation. Why do you want to take up meditation? The bottom line is this: if you want to meditate, you have to make time to do it. Do you have time to heal your life?

Meditation is too boring.

When people complain that meditation is too boring, they usually have some unreasonable expectations about what meditation can do for them. Or they have a mistaken idea of what meditation is.

In mindfulness practice, you should investigate whatever is here. This calls for a willingness to allow yourself to experience whatever is happening, including the feeling of boredom. Can you breathe into the experience and stay present with it? Allow it to unfold and reveal itself. Boredom often has elements of negative judgment and self-talk. There is frustration that can actually be felt in the body, and aversion for some aspect of what is present. The next time you feel "bored" in your meditation, try to take a closer look at what is actually going on. What you discover will not be boring.

When I sit still and meditate, it makes me more anxious.

Isn't that interesting? Do you think that it might be possible that you are not actually more anxious, but that by stopping and sitting still, you have become *more aware* of the anxiety that is already present? In meditation, you have dropped the habits of inattention, distraction, and absence that have kept you out of touch with the anxiety. You are more mindful of it now.

To master the feelings of worry, anxiety, and panic, you must understand them. This does not mean merely having more thoughts or information about the feelings. Some thoughts and information are necessary, but you must also understand the experience directly from the inside as it unfolds and develops. This experiential learning aspect is integral to the mindfulness approach. You are learning what it means to work with the agitated mind by being there with kind and focused awareness while it happens. You are learning to recognize and not fall victim to the reactivity of your own mind in the face of such intense states as worry and anxiety. So when anxiety arises in your meditation, remember that you have not done anything wrong. Just breathe into the anxiety and the situation, and make the anxiety experience itself the object of your attention and awareness. See if you can make enough inner space around the experience to allow it to unfold.

But I don't like the feeling. I want to get away from it. I don't want to feel it anymore.

That is understandable. Anyone dealing with the unpleasantness and disruption of chronic fear or anxiety has those feelings of aversion and desire for relief. But have you ever really been able to get away from the anxiety? Or has your life become a constant state of monitoring the mind and body for any trace of anxiety's return? Have you become anxious about the anxiety? Has the anxiety, in whatever form, become an enemy in your own mind and body? Do you feel at war in your own mind and body?

At some point in dealing with chronic conditions of pain, stress, fear, or anxiety, almost everyone feels this way. This is where the practices of kindness and compassion for yourself, and the capacity for deep relaxation and relief through concentration on the breath and through the body-focused practices, are very useful.

When such dislike and ill will for the anxiety is present, please recognize that it is your relationship to anxiety that must change before anything else can. This means stopping the war and being willing to be present and allow what is happening.

One way I like to practice mindfulness is by the simple instruction "relax and stay present."

The first and most difficult task in working with such intense disruptions as anxiety and panic is simply establishing and maintaining attention in a relaxed and calm way. It is very difficult to remain present and mindful when there is great upset and tension. By concentrating attention and by using kindness and compassion for yourself in a skillful way, you can strengthen relaxation and attention, and awareness can become more clear.

Recognize and accept that things are this way—now. Then work in practical ways to take care of yourself and to comfort yourself just as you would your own child or a friend who was in distress. Stop the negative self-talk and the critical commentary. If it won't stop, allow it. See it as only more thinking—nothing else. Then use the body scan, walking meditation or other mindful movement, or breath awareness to focus attention and to find the stillness and spaciousness that is also present in this moment.

Practice mindful breathing as the situation is happening. Breathe with awareness in and out, over, under, and through the anxiety and allow the cradle of the breath to hold all that is present. Let that place of inner stillness become the container for the agitated mind and all of the aversion and despair that has accumulated there.

I'm sorry, but I just can't seem to sit still. I am just so anxious. Am I too anxious to meditate?

This is not an unusual feeling or an uncommon question. The short answer is no, you are not too anxious to meditate. The long answer involves something more. It is related to what we talked about in the previous question.

The first thing to remember is that the truth about anxiety and worry, even about panic, is that they are not you. They are actually only conditions that flow in and out of the present moment. Confusion arises when the intensity of these conditions leads you to begin to identify with them and become lost in a reaction to them. Remember how the mind and body communicate and feed each other? This is what is happening.

A core principle of meditative disciplines is to establish calm and focused attention. What this means is that when you are feeling overwhelmed by anxiety, you must find some way to focus mindful attention in the present moment. This usually means establishing and reestablishing attention.

In this book we have worked extensively using awareness of the breath sensation as the vehicle for establishing and maintaining the connection with the present moment. You have practiced breathing in and out with whatever is happening. This conscious breathing, practiced with what is happening, establishes a focus of attention in the present moment and links the mind and body together with the unfolding experience. It allows for a softening and opening that does not try to change the experience, but instead permits it to be what it is.

The method you use to establish calm and focused attention is not as important as that you do it. For example, sometimes you may be able to establish attention by practicing mindful breathing. At other times, you may have to do some kind of mindful movement like walking meditation or yoga before you can sustain attention on the experience that is happening.

When you are able to observe the anxiety with a better focus, the anxiety itself can be the object of mindfulness. You will be able to allow the sensations and thoughts more easily without becoming lost in them or reacting to them. You will have broken your identification with them, and this will allow you to respond rather than react to them.

It all begins with establishing calm and focused attention.

I don't think I have the discipline to meditate. It's just not for me.

Challenge yourself to take a closer look at what you are saying to yourself. What is present in your own mind and heart when those thoughts arise?

When people say they don't have the discipline to meditate, it's usually because they have tried to meditate but obstacles have come up. The demands of their life and the habits of inattention, distraction, and absence have roared back at them. Self-doubt usually follows that roar. People begin to doubt their own ability and strength to deal with the obstacles.

Remember that mindfulness, kindness, and compassion are allies. The practices act as a friend to accompany you and help you deal with the challenges you meet in life. You don't have to be "perfect" at doing the meditation. There is nothing to attain. Just doing the practices is good enough. Work with them and learn how and where they fit in your life. You will change, the practices will change, circumstances will change. Just relax and work with them now, as best you can.

Let go of any thoughts of perfection or bliss or becoming the perfect mindfulness meditation person. When obstacles arise, learn to note them. Let them be, without identifying with them or believing them. That really is all you need to do.

It doesn't work for me. I can't get it right.

Listen to yourself, mindfully. What is the tone of voice of that statement? What feelings are present inside when you look deeply with kind awareness?

This concern represents a very common experience for almost everyone who takes up meditation (or anything else). The experience is one of inaccurate and unrealistic expectations followed by harsh judgment and waves of self-criticism, frustration, and despair.

These are some more of those strong habits that are completely revealed by the light of mindfulness. When they arise in you, just note them. Let them be. Let the thoughts, or the sensations, or whatever become the object of mindfulness. Practice kindness and acceptance for what is inside you in this moment.

Questions about Specific Meditation Practices

I don't have time to do everything as slowly as I ate that raisin. Does this mean I can't be mindful?

Mindfulness is not dependent on speed. The power to be present is already in you. In the practices, like the raisin exercise, we guide you very slowly for another reason.

Although mindfulness is already in you, the habits of inattention and absence are present also. The speed at which you move through activities and experiences often reflects inattention and a sense of hurriedness that have become habits of living. All of us have gotten into habits of inattention that interfere with being mindful. If you are not paying attention in the first place, you will find it hard to be aware of what is here.

To establish attention and maintain it takes some effort. By slowing down any activity and concentrating attention in as much detail as possible, you are teaching yourself to be more present. As you develop the art of attention, you will discover that you can be more present moving at faster speeds. You can always establish mindfulness, in any activity, moving at any speed. It starts with paying attention.

Practicing awareness of breathing, body scan, or even walking meditation, I am bothered that my mind is all over the place. I can't seem to control my thoughts.

Isn't that interesting? Where did you get the idea you should control your thoughts?

In mindfulness practices, it is good enough to recognize that you are having the thoughts. That is a moment of mindfulness. Just work with the thoughts by recognizing them. In the practices you mentioned, you are practicing maintaining a focus on the breath, the body, or the activity of walking. When thoughts (or other distractions) arise, just notice them, let them be, and return the focus to your primary object of meditation.

In meditation practice, the thoughts are treated like anything else: just something to notice. In the practice of choiceless awareness, you actually make the thoughts themselves the object as long as they are present. Hold the commentary, or the pictures, or whatever form thoughts take, in the light of mindfulness, breathing in and out with them, listening and watching them. You can literally experience them as arising, changing, and leaving. They are not you, no matter how dramatic, compelling, or important they seem.

Either way, by letting the thoughts be and returning awareness to breath or body, or by making the thoughts themselves the object, you are no longer identifying with them. Nor are you adding to them with more thoughts. You are simply recognizing that they are happening and letting them be.

In the body scan, sometimes I love it because I get so relaxed. Other times I hate it because I can't sit still, or I fall asleep, or I don't think it is working.

Do you see how much liking and disliking depend upon feeling comfortable, or upon things going as you think they should? It is fine to feel comfortable, and to have ideas about things. But can you look more deeply?

Meditation practice empowers you to recognize how these habits of seeking comfort and answers, along with the judging they require, can be a source of pain. The pain can appear as fear of losing security, worry or anxiety about keeping security, or some variation on these themes.

The body scan practice is about connecting with and becoming more aware of the body, just as it is. While this does lead to relaxation, and while relaxation is important, the relaxation is not the ultimate goal. Awareness is. Try not to judge your practice by how relaxed or "good" you feel. Try not to judge it at all. Just try to be present and to recognize and accept what is here. Notice how things change from day to day, from practice to practice. Don't try to hold on or to make anything happen.

Practicing choiceless awareness, I get lost easily. Anxiety is strong, my mind fills with frightening thoughts, and I worry that I am losing control of everything. What should I do?

This is a very good question. Feeling lost, filled with anxiety, and out of control are common and intense experiences. Do not become discouraged. This happens at times to practically everyone who takes up meditation.

In fact, meditation exists to help you manage exactly these situations. As you practice and encounter these difficult visitors in meditation, you are learning how to manage them with awareness and kindness. What you learn will help you whenever and wherever the difficult ones appear.

We will discuss working with fear, anxiety, and panic in more detail in the next chapter.

The basic principles are simple, but not often easy!

〜 Establish and maintain attention in the present moment. As we have been practicing, this means establishing awareness on the breath and then breathing in and out with whatever is happening. We have called this *holding it in the cradle of the breath.*

〜 With attention established, and mind, body, and present moment connected through conscious breathing, make the unfolding experience itself the object of mindfulness.

Bring your curious and allowing attention deeply to whatever experience is present.

Once you have established attention on the breath, you are no longer lost. Start breathing into the feelings of anxiety in the body and let the feelings themselves be the object of mindfulness. Listen to the worried and frightening thoughts and let them be, and let the fear of losing control become the next condition you hold in kind awareness.

Remember, all of this is arising, changing, and leaving in the present moment. Your practice is to remain present with kind attention as these visitors come and go. That is peaceful abiding. And it takes practice! It may take time and effort for concentration and mindfulness to become strong enough that you aren't lost or overwhelmed by the array of thoughts and feelings. That is okay. Take all the time you need. Just keep practicing.

When I practice the loving-kindness meditation, usually I don't feel much. It seems phony. I even get angry, or sometimes sad. I don't get it. Is something wrong with me?

These are excellent observations, and it is a very good question. No, there is absolutely nothing wrong with you. These are very common feelings that arise when people begin to practice the meditations on kindness and compassion.

This practice of loving-kindness is about connecting with something you already have. The qualities of kindness and compassion are in everyone. That you are having difficulty feeling them is actually very common.

The same habits of inattention and absence that interfere with mindfulness also work to block you from feeling your own capacity for kindness, and from realizing your compassionate connection with life. Further, the habits of meanness, driven by anger and hostility, are deep. Indeed, the anger and hostility are often fed on a deeper level by fear and feelings of separation and abandonment.

As you teach yourself the art of attention and are able to connect more deeply with the present moment, you will find that you will be able to hear the words of the loving-kindness meditation practice more clearly, and will begin to feel them in your mind and body more easily. It just takes practice.

As your meditation practice deepens, don't be surprised if more feelings of anger or sadness appear. With deep listening and connection comes deep release and healing. Strong feelings of anger or sadness often are simply waiting to be released. Your kind and compassionate attention gives them release. Healing and transformation is happening.

I have trouble finding an image of myself when doing the loving-kindness practice. What should I do?

This is an excellent question. Almost everyone who begins the loving-kindness practice has difficulty sending kindness to themselves.

Try to relax and connect with some part of yourself that you can feel or picture. If you are having difficulty, it can help to focus attention on your own body as you practice. Simply send kindness there.

Also, you aren't restricted to a "total" image of yourself. You could focus on a region of your body, perhaps one that is injured or ill. Or you could focus on part of your emotional or cognitive body, like anger, anxiety, or constant judging.

As your practice deepens and sensitivity grows, you will discover new dimensions within. This will lead to new ways to practice kindness for yourself and for others.

chapter 14

applying mindfulness to fear and anxiety

In an interview with Jon Kabat-Zinn published in *Healing and the Mind*, Bill Moyers (1993) asked about the purpose of meditation. Kabat-Zinn responded, "There is no purpose in meditation. As soon as you assign a purpose to meditation, you've made it just another activity to try to get someplace or reach some goal. (p. 128)"

When questioned further, Kabat-Zinn explained that yes, everyone in the mindfulness-based stress reduction program had a purpose for being there, "but paradoxically, they are likely to make the most progress in this domain if they let go of trying to get anywhere and just learn through the practice of meditation to experience their moments as they unfold. (p. 129)"

Developing a Skillful Approach to Fear and Anxiety

Probably you are reading this book because you are seeking help for the fear, anxiety, or panic you experience. You have a definite purpose and goal. And most likely, you have done and continue to do everything you can to understand these forces and to manage them or even eliminate them in your life. Perhaps someone told you to learn to meditate to rid yourself of anxiety or panic. All of this is fine and understandable.

The Paradox of Meditation

The catch is that if you are trying to use mindfulness to get rid of something, it doesn't work. Mindfulness is nonjudging, nonstriving, and nondenying. The practice of mindfulness is about connecting with what is here and holding it in kind and compassionate awareness. This includes the experiences of fear, anxiety, and panic.

So if you have a "secret agenda" of using mindfulness against anxiety or panic, remind yourself that mindfulness involves accepting what is here. Having an agenda to get rid of something or to change something is a common source of frustration in meditation practice. Change and transformation do occur through meditation, but only when you teach yourself to allow attention and awareness to include disturbing and unpleasant conditions like anxiety and panic.

In the domain of meditation, it is the practice of being, not doing, that works. To be skillful in approaching any distress in your life—

including fear, anxiety, or panic—through meditation, it is helpful to recall some fundamental points.

~~ Everything happens in the present moment.

~~ Fear, anxiety, and panic are only experiences flowing into and out of the present moment.

~~ Meditation can be understood as a process of inner transformation that involves establishing a calm and focused attention, cultivating awareness, developing understanding and wisdom, and activating kindness and compassion.

~~ By correctly practicing mindfulness of fear, anxiety, and panic, you develop a clear understanding of their lesson and begin to see what action is necessary.

Again, there is the paradox. To produce change through meditation, you have to stop trying to change anything! It is good enough to be present. It is strong practice to bring full attention to the present moment—*as it is*. Doing this, you actually touch the mystery and beauty of life and resonate with it. Change and transformation follow from this contact and awareness.

Accepting Disturbing Experiences

Fear, anxiety, and panic are demanding visitors. They can turn your inner world upside down. It can be difficult to be allowing and accepting of them because of their intense and disturbing nature. Are there practical ways to deal with such disturbing experiences in meditation?

The final answer to this question comes through your own direct experience in making meditation a part of your life. You will need to practice mindfulness in different ways as a formal daily meditation, and without trying to get anywhere or accomplish anything other than becoming more mindful. You will also need to bring mindfulness forward as an informal practice by remembering to establish and maintain attention and awareness in the situations of daily life.

With this foundation of mindfulness in your life, whenever fear, anxiety, or panic arises, you will have the tools to manage it. Only through your own experience of using mindfulness to work with these powerful forces will you discover what works best for you.

Working Mindfully with Fear

Your father is in the intensive care unit on a ventilator, somewhere between life and death. You visit him and feel overwhelmed. You are facing fear.

You have just learned that the test results from your colonoscopy show that you have cancer. You are stunned. You are facing fear.

You have just come from a meeting with your supervisor. Your job is being eliminated by the company for "budgetary reasons." You are angry and confused. You are facing fear.

You dread flying, yet you are about to board an airplane. You are flying because of a family emergency. You are facing fear.

The list of examples is endless. When you really pay attention, the experience of fear seems to be everywhere in modern life. In most cases, you know exactly why you feel afraid, yet you must still deal with the fear.

How can you use mindfulness and compassion to approach the fear in your life? In the remainder of this chapter, we will reflect on practicing specifically with fear, anxiety, and panic. There are no easy answers. Much of meditation practice involves patience and the willingness to be with distress and discomfort. Practice is about learning to find the place inside where there is ease and calm in the midst of upset. The following reflections come from the experiences of many people who have practiced mindfulness this way.

Remind yourself that mindfulness accurately reflects what is here. To say to yourself "This is fear" is a start. "Fear is like this." "It is like this now." Acknowledging what is here establishes presence and names what is here. This acknowledgment interrupts the habit of unconscious reaction to the fearful situation. By continuing to notice in this way, you will also notice when fear changes or is absent. Fear is not permanent. Fear is not you. These truths will also become obvious as you note what is here.

Establish and maintain a calm and focused attention. There are many ways to establish attention in the present moment. In this book I have emphasized using breathing. Focus attention on your breathing, as in the meditation practice for awareness of breathing you learned in chapter 9. This means breathing with the unfolding experience, not trying to run back to the breath or to hide there. Practice consciously breathing in and out with the fear experience. The body scan meditation also involves breathing with experience, and the breath is the anchor for the choiceless awareness practice.

The other core principles of meditation—awareness, understanding, and compassion—can flourish once calm and focused attention is established and maintained. Indeed, in working with fear and fearful situations, maintaining connection and attention is usually the most difficult task.

If you are afraid of snakes, rats, or spiders, when you encounter one, try breathing consciously and staying with what is happening (even as you make sure you distance yourself safely).

If you fear crowds, or open spaces, or closed spaces and find yourself there anyway, recognize what is happening. Establish connection with the breath or the body. Breathe consciously as you have practiced, into and out of the situation, establishing and reestablishing your calm and focused attention on what is unfolding.

Try mindful movement. Walking meditation, mindful yoga, tai chi, chi kung, and mindful exercise are all examples. You will need to experiment to discover what works best to help you stay present. The more solid and confident you are in your movement practice, the more it will help you. This is why grounding yourself in a daily practice as a way of living is the most effective way for practice to help you in times of urgent need.

Be willing to persevere. You may have to do your conscious breathing or mindful movement for quite a while when dealing with the fear response. Staying with the situation this way strengthens concentration and mindfulness.

This calls for patience and endurance. Just stay with it anyway. There is a place for simply enduring. It will strengthen your meditation practice. Over time, you will recognize your increased power to be present.

Cultivate allowing and nonjudging awareness. With attention established, allowing and nonjudging awareness can rest on and include all elements present in the fear situation. Mindfulness includes all that is here. The unfolding experience of the body, the thoughts and stories in the mind: these are of particular importance to note. No matter how intense or disturbing, these should be treated as simply more conditions present in this moment. Here again, it is easy to become lost or absorbed in the fear experiences. Breathing into them and holding them in the cradle of the breath helps you maintain the focus and connection, and realize the truth that these experiences are not you and are not permanent.

Remember that mindfulness is spacious and light. Mindfulness does not attach to anything. It is easy to allow yourself to be absorbed by a fearful reaction. It is easy to identify with and to react to fear. If you are feeling stuck in the fear, try opening the awareness to the space around the feeling. Try opening attention to include sounds or other sensations. This is similar to practicing the body scan and opening awareness to the entire body beyond a particular region.

Alternatively, try focusing more sharply on the elements of the experience: the exact location of the sensation in the body, the very beginning of the fearful thought or negative commentary, or the precise ending of each sensation, thought, or other element.

Thus, by opening awareness to include the fear experience, you dissolve your identification with it. Similarly, you can break the identification with the fear experience by narrowing attention to a smaller part of the experience.

Welcome the understanding and wisdom that grow from seeing clearly. No matter what causes your fear, the most effective response comes from a clear understanding of the situation and of all your choices. As you stay present and manage the tendencies to fight or to flee from your fear, you will open to more choices for action. This will lead to more effective action and to a greater confidence that you can handle difficult, fearful situations.

Have kindness and compassion for yourself and your fear. If you have practiced loving-kindness meditation enough to have some confidence in doing it, this meditation can be a great support in times of fear.

May I be happy. May I be healthy. May I be filled with peace and ease. May I be safe. Kindling the feelings of kindness and compassion using these phrases or others, you support presence and awareness.

When you feel overwhelmed and distressed, gently caring for yourself with feelings of friendliness and compassion is very grounding and soothing. You can feel something inside relax and soften as you practice kindness. It becomes easier to relax and to stay present. It becomes easier to observe and listen mindfully to the unfolding experience.

Working Mindfully with Anxiety and Worry

You have a job and a good circle of friends, yet you are bothered frequently by vague feelings of fear and dread. These feelings leave you upset and afraid you will lose control of yourself in public places. You have begun to decline invitations and dates because of this fear of losing control. You are now filled with anxiety about what might happen and what you fear you cannot do.

You are afraid of groups, and terrified of speaking in front of groups. You fear you will embarrass or humiliate yourself. You recognize that you have no reason to feel so anxious, but you do anyway. You are avoiding situations—including job opportunities—that would require you to speak in front of lots of people. You are becoming angry at yourself and feeling more anxious.

You have been anxious and worried most of the time for over six months. You worry most of the day about the stressful parts of your life. In the last six months, this has included your health, your marriage, your job, and the care of your elderly mother. You are often restless, tire easily, and have not slept well in weeks. You have anxiety about what might happen, and cannot stop worrying about things that have not happened and probably won't happen.

The experience of anxiety and worry is very common and very disturbing. However it is expressed in your life, it requires attention. How can you approach anxiety and worry skillfully with mindfulness and compassion?

Laying the Groundwork

You will do best if you build your mindfulness practice on a solid foundation. Especially when anxiety and worry are your focus, a careful assessment of causes, treatment possibilities, and the role of your own lifestyle choices is critical.

Treatments

There are many effective treatments for anxiety. Be sure to have a good medical and psychological assessment if anxiety is excessive or disturbing in your life. Meditation is a strong ally but is not a substitute for good treatment.

Life Circumstances

Bring mindful attention to every corner of your own life circumstances. Is anything about your personal life, relationships, or work life adding to your anxiety? Can you change it? How? Consider talking this over with your spouse or a trusted friend, and invite their input.

Habits

Don't forget personal habits. This includes what you eat, drink, or take in through any other form. It definitely includes the use of alcohol, drugs, or medications. Include also what you take in from mass media and entertainment sources. Without judging anything, simply begin to pay attention to what you do and absorb, and how that makes you feel. When you have identified sources of anxiety, you are ready to make changes for the better.

Daily Mindfulness Practice

After laying this groundwork, you are in the best position for your daily meditation practice to help. And as you do your daily mindfulness practice, formally or informally, it will support you in relaxing, seeing clearly, and in making effective changes.

Mindfulness is not a method, but a way of living. What this means is that mindfulness helps you the most when you make a daily meditation practice the foundation for developing mindfulness in your life.

The goal of your practice is simply to open to what is present with increasing sensitivity and clarity. Meditation teacher Joseph Goldstein (1993) puts this succinctly:

> Our progress in meditation does not depend on the measure of pleasure or pain in our experience. Rather, the quality of our practice has to do with how open we are to whatever is there. . . .
>
> What we have experienced in the past is gone. Be watchful that you are not holding on to some past experience that you are trying to re-create. That is not correct practice; it is a sure setup for suffering. Simply be open, be soft, be mindful with whatever is presenting itself. (p. 47)

The methods of mindfulness you use in daily practice will change, and so will the emphasis. The core activity does not change. With mindfulness you are embarking on a path of awakening and transformation. You are coming off of automatic pilot and embracing life consciously.

Learning from Anxiety and Worry

Fear, anxiety, and panic contain information about you and how you meet your life. What is to be learned? Be curious. Curiosity and investigation empower you to discover the lessons of what Joan Halifax (1993) calls the "fruitful darkness." These are the lessons that fear, anxiety, and panic can teach you about living.

In meditation practice, you approach worry and anxiety—fear without a clearly identifiable cause—the same way you approach fear that does have an identifiable cause. As you practice, make the worry and anxiety the direct object of attention. Maintain contact lightly without becoming absorbed by the story or feeling. Use mindful breathing, in and out with the experience, to stay connected.

As with fear, establishing and maintaining conscious contact with the experience of anxiety or worry is often the most difficult part. It is easy to get swept into reaction and identification, or dissociation from the experience, because of its unpleasant and disturbing nature.

Choosing the Foundation for Your Practice

People often ask which kinds of practices are best matched with which types of anxiety. For example, does a person who experiences anxiety "in the head" (as worrying and obsessive thinking) need a different type of relaxation exercise or meditation practice than the person who experiences anxiety mostly "in the body" (as feelings of restlessness or other discomfort)?

Although some research has addressed this question, the findings are not conclusive and in some cases are even contradictory. Of value to mindfulness practitioners, however, is a report published by Kabat-Zinn and colleagues (1997) in the journal *Mind/Body Medicine.*

In a study of seventy-four patients with elevated levels of anxiety, those with "high cognitive/low somatic" scores (those who experienced anxiety mostly "in the head") preferred somatic (body-focused) mindfulness practice. The "high somatic/low cognitive" anxiety group (those who experienced anxiety mostly "in the body") showed the inverse response: they preferred the sitting meditation. Both groups preferred the body scan, which includes both cognitive and somatic qualities, to an intermediate degree. It would be unwise to form rigid ideas based on this study; however, the results do have an interesting implication.

Mindfulness practice is most effective when it includes the mental *and* the physical experience. Therefore, you should have meditation practices that emphasize both in your daily practice. What the methods are is not so important as the quality of attention paid to mind *and* body in a systematic and consistent manner.

If you experience anxiety mostly in your head (that is, if you are a "worrier"), then you might want to experiment with movement practices as a foundation for mindfulness. Alternatively, you might want to begin each formal session of meditation with some movement before sitting meditation. The movement practices could be whatever appeals or is available to you: walking meditation, mindful exercise, yoga, tai chi, chi kung, or something else.

Also, developing the skill of connecting with your body by using the body scan practice is likely to be a great help for you. In general, restoring attentional balance by moving out of the head and into the body more often is worth exploring.

If you are bothered more by the physical expression of anxiety, then you may benefit by emphasizing sitting practice. Breath awareness meditation and choiceless awareness meditation are good places to start. In addition, your sitting meditation should always include the bodily experience. You apply mindfulness to your body in doing the body scan, and also in the choiceless awareness practice as you include bodily sensations.

Whether you experience anxiety primarily in your head or in your body, you will probably benefit also by doing the loving-kindness and compassion meditation. This calms and relaxes your mind and body through concentration of attention on phrase repetition, and it can awaken you to a larger context of relatedness to life. This larger-vessel perspective is a good balance to the self-involvement and absorption that follows so much of anxiety and worry.

Applying Mindfulness to Panic Attacks and Intense Fear

The intensity that accompanies panic attacks is almost indescribable. If you are subject to these attacks, please apply the basic approach first. This means seeking good treatment, analyzing your own life situation, developing a daily meditation practice, and making the panic experience itself the object of mindfulness.

Then, you might experiment with the following.

Remember that in intense situations, establishing and maintaining conscious contact with the unfolding experience is usually the most difficult task. The tendency is to be overwhelmed in the experience and swept away in reactivity to the unpleasantness. This can happen in your bodily sensations, in your thoughts, and in your behavior.

Your practice is to make the actual experience of the attack the object of mindful attention. Hold it in view, establishing and maintaining contact without becoming identified with it or absorbed into it.

Steady and ground yourself by acknowledging what is happening. Name the panic.

Center attention using mindful breathing, and concentrate your attention as you allow the body experience to unfold, breathing with it and into it.

Listen to the fearful thoughts mindfully. Recognize them as merely more thoughts. Breathe with them. Allow them without believing them or arguing with them. If they are too intense and loud, try to breathe with them with sharper concentration on the breath. Or try moving attention to the body or to sounds in the environment.

Use kindness and compassion for yourself and for the panic elements themselves, whether they are in your body or mind. Remember "May I be filled with peace and ease. May I be safe."

You may have already developed techniques like using affirmations (making encouraging comments to yourself). Use these to steady yourself if necessary. Stay connected. Keep the panic experience in view, but beware of becoming sucked into it. You will have to practice with the methods of attention, awareness, and kindness in order to learn how to apply these skills to the direct experience of panic most effectively.

Keep in Mind

Remember, you *do* have what it takes. You *can* find the inner calm and peace you need. You *can* change things by paying attention.

The paradox is that you practice meditation with *no* goal in order to reach your goal of managing anxiety, fear, and panic.

By bringing a kind and compassionate attention to the experiences of fear, anxiety, and panic, you make them the objects of mindfulness. Meeting these experiences with nonjudging, curious attention is all you have to do to access the power of mindfulness.

chapter 15

taking a
larger view

The intrusive and painful experiences of fear, anxiety, and panic have a way of shrinking your view of yourself and your place in the world. Indeed, this is true of any form of pain or challenge that stops you in your tracks and demands that you pay attention to it above all else.

As the demands persist, becoming chronic as well as intense, you might come to feel as if you are in a prison. Life itself seems to shrink into compartments. *What I can do* and *where I can go* becomes less and less, smaller and smaller.

These thoughts and feelings of restriction and "fear about the fear" can become powerful even than the intense experience of fear in the body.

The tendency to identify with the fear or anxiety grows as the feelings themselves strengthen. "I am anxious" or "I am afraid" becomes not only a self-description but an identity. Reactivity to the pain becomes the pervasive experience in life.

In these ways, fear, anxiety, and panic have become a prison. And the prisoner is the person who somehow feels less competent, less effective, less alive than before.

The message of this book is that you can be free of the prison of fear, anxiety, and panic. The keys to freedom lie within you. They operate as you teach yourself to bring full attention to life.

From the view of mindfulness, everything happens in the present moment. The experiences of life are flowing, even now, through the present moment. This includes the powerful inner experiences of fear, anxiety, and panic. These experiences are not permanent, and they are not who you are. Your connection with life has not ceased. You are not as isolated as it seems.

Recovering the Sense of Connection to Life

Healing is a process of making whole. For this to happen, all the parts that are separate and isolated or denied must be brought into awareness and included. This is true in healing individual people and in the healing of larger bodies such as communities or nations.

Psychotherapists have long held that this process of healing requires you to experience, accept, and take responsibility for the dark side of yourself. The dark side includes all the things that are fearsome, embarrassing, shame-filled, and the like. In short, the things you don't want to know and vigorously deny about yourself. It also includes those inner energies and forces that you feel powerless to control. The process of healing makes inquiry into this valley of darkness vital. Yet most people do not enter this inquiry willingly.

John Tarrant is a well-known Zen teacher and Jungian psychotherapist. In *The Light inside the Dark* (1998), he speaks of this descent into the darkness:

> The journey into a life of awareness begins for most of us in a moment of helplessness. When our lives are going well, we do not feel any need to change them, or ourselves. . . . We are unperturbed, and half asleep. Then a crisis arrives . . . strips us of everything we have relied upon to stay the same. Yet this unexpected fall is also a gift, not to be refused. . . . We realize that we have no choice: before we can rise up, we must go down and through. (p. 27)

The experiences of fear, anxiety, or panic may well have been the crisis that has driven you down into the darkness. Yet they also hold the promise of awakening into a life of greater awareness if you can manage them and learn from them. The pain you associate with them can be the link to a deeper self-understanding and to a broader connectedness with the life of the world around you.

Joan Halifax (1993), a respected Buddhist teacher and anthropologist, speaks in *The Fruitful Darkness* to the interrelatedness of life through painful experience:

> My suffering is not unique but arises out of the ground of my culture. It arises out of the global culture and environment as well. I am part of the World's Body. If part of this body is suffering, then the world suffers.
>
> Recognizing the World Wound also turns us away from a sense of exclusiveness. . . . Each of us carries or has carried suffering. This suffering is personal. But where is it that we end and the rest of creation begins? (p. 13–14)

To recognize that the pain I feel in me is the same pain that you feel in you is to arrive at the heart of compassion and kindness. To begin to understand that the pain inside is not so much about you, in some self-centered way, as it is about a call to respond and relate to a larger context of life is to begin to awaken. These are messages that make more sense as you use mindfulness to connect with the moments of your life.

Meditation practiced correctly has no purpose other than to transform and awaken us. In connecting with the wholeness of experience in this moment, you are able to discover what matters most. The mystery and the beauty of living are experienced directly. Understanding and wisdom follow this direct experience.

Meditation does not tell you what meaning life has. It allows you to discover the meaning for yourself. Indeed, no one can tell you what meaning life has for you.

Meaning must be discovered by listening and connecting with increasing sensitivity in each moment. It comes from asking What is the lesson in this experience? Can you begin to ask that question about the fear, anxiety, or panic in your life?

Viktor Frankl survived Nazi concentration camps including Auschwitz. His experiences there led him to develop a form of psychotherapy he called *logotherapy.* The name is taken from the Greek word *logos,* which denotes "meaning." Logotherapy focuses on the meaning of human existence and on each human being's search for meaning as a primary motivational force in life. This approach puts a person immediately in a larger context beyond the small, ego-driven view of the world. As Frankl (1959) stated in *Man's Search for Meaning,* "Ultimately, man should not ask what the meaning of his life is, but rather must recognize that it is *he* who is asked. In a word, each man is questioned by life; and he can only answer to life by *answering for* his own life; to life he can only respond by being responsible. (p. 172)"

Can you move beyond the idea of fear, anxiety, and panic as intruders or enemies? Can you find the lessons of transformation they hold? Can you discover your interconnection with others through the pain of anxiety and panic? Can you find a deeper meaning and purpose by taking Frankl's approach and considering what question life is asking you through fear, anxiety, or panic?

As you teach yourself to connect with and remain present in the moments of your life, the lessons, transformations, questions, and answers will begin to reveal themselves to you.

Come Here, Fear

To hold fear, or anxiety, or panic with kindness and compassion is powerful. The ability to do this comes from the understanding that they are not you, but are only experiences and conditions flowing into and out of the present moment. The pain and suffering they carry is only momentary experience. Yet that pain also calls for kindness and compassion.

The poet Joy Harjo speaks to this new relationship with fear in her beautiful poem "I Give You Back."

> I take myself back, fear.
> You are not my shadow any longer.
> I won't hold you in my hands.
> You can't live in my eyes, my ears, my voice
> my belly, or in my heart my heart
> my heart my heart
> But come here, fear
> I am alive and you are so afraid
> of dying.

It is my deep hope that you will be able to use this book to establish your own practice of mindfulness.

May it grow and sustain you.

May you find peace and calm as a result.

May that practice awaken your heart of kindness and compassion.

May clarity and understanding follow in all your days.

May mindfulness and compassion free you from anxiety, fear, and panic.

resources

Books on Meditation and Mindfulness

Feldman, Christina. 1998. *Thorsons Principles of Meditation*. London: Thorsons.

Glassman, Bernie. 1998. *Bearing Witness: A Zen Master's Lessons in Making Peace*. New York: Bell Tower.

Goldstein, Joseph. 1993. *Insight Meditation*. Boston: Shambhala.

Gunaratana, Henepola. 1994. *Mindfulness in Plain English*. Boston: Wisdom Publications.

Kabat-Zinn, Jon. 1990. *Full Catastrophe Living*. New York: Delacorte Press.

Kabat-Zinn, Jon. 1994. *Wherever You Go, There You Are*. New York: Hyperion.

Kornfield, Jack. 1993. *A Path with Heart*. New York: Bantam.

Kornfield, Jack, and Joseph Goldstein. 1987. *Seeking the Heart of Wisdom*. Boston: Shambhala.

Levine, Stephen. 1979. *A Gradual Awakening*. Garden City, N.Y.: Anchor Books.

Rosenberg, Larry. 1998. *Breath by Breath*. Boston: Shambhala.

Salzberg, Sharon. 1995. *Loving-Kindness: The Revolutionary Art of Happiness*. Boston: Shambhala.

Salzberg, Sharon. 1997. *A Heart as Wide as the World*. Boston: Shambhala.

Santorelli, Saki. 1999. *Heal Thyself.* New York: Bell Tower.

Thich Nhat Hanh. 1975. *The Miracle of Mindfulness*. Boston: Beacon Press.

Thich Nhat Hanh. 1987. *Being Peace*. Berkeley, Calif.: Parallax Press.

Meditation Recordings

Sounds True in Boulder, Colorado, has a wonderful collection. Contact them at (800) 333-9185 or www.soundstrue.com (click on "store," then click on "meditation and prayer").

Books on Yoga

Feuerstein, Georg, and Stephan Bodian, with the staff of *Yoga Journal*. 1993. *Living Yoga: A Comprehensive Guide for Everyday Life*. New York: Tarcher/Putnam.

Francina, Suza. 1997. *The New Yoga for People over 50.* Deerfield Beach, Fla.: Health Communications, Inc.

Johnson, Will. 2000. *Aligned, Relaxed, Resilient: The Physical Foundations of Mindfulness.* Boston: Shambhala.

Yoga Videos and DVDs

Yoga Journal's instructional videotapes and DVDs are widely available in bookstores, online, and in health product stores.

Mindfulness-Based Stress Reduction Programs

The author is the director of the Mindfulness-Based Stress Reduction Program in the Duke Center for Integrative Medicine. The program may be contacted by mail at: MBSR Program, DUMC 3022, Durham, NC 27710; by phone at (919) 660-6745; or on the Web at *www.dcim.org.*

Mindfulness-based stress reduction was developed at the University of Massachusetts Medical Center. The director of that program is Saki Santorelli. You may contact the program by mail at: Stress Reduction Clinic, University of Massachusetts Medical Center, 55 Lake Avenue North, Worcester, MA 01005 or by phone at (508) 856-2656.

You may also locate mindfulness-based stress reduction programs by Internet search using *MBSR* or *mindfulness-based stress reduction* as your key words.

references

Albom, M. 1997. *Tuesdays with Morrie.* New York: Doubleday.

American Psychiatric Association. 1994. *Diagnostic and Statistical Manual of Mental Disorders,* 4th ed. Washington, D.C.: American Psychiatric Association.

Astin, J. 1997. Stress reduction through mindfulness meditation: Effects on psychological symptomatology, sense of control, and spiritual experiences. *Psychotherapy and Psychosomatics* 66:97–106.

Benson, H. 1993. The relaxation response. In *Mind Body Medicine,* edited by D. Goleman and J. Gurin. New York: Consumer Reports Books.

Bourne, E. 2000. *The Anxiety and Phobia Workbook.* Oakland, Calif.: New Harbinger.

Chodron, P. 2001. *The Places That Scare You.* Boston: Shambhala.

Feldman, C. 1998. *Thorsons Principles of Meditation.* London: Thorsons.

———. 2001. *The Buddhist Path to Simplicity.* London: Thorsons.

Frankl, V. 1959. *Man's Search for Meaning.* New York: Pocket Books.

Freeman, L., and G. F. Lawlis. 2001. *Mosby's Complementary and Alternative Medicine: A Research-Based Approach.* St. Louis: Mosby.

Goldstein, J. 1993. *Insight Meditation.* Boston: Shambhala.

Goleman, D. 2003. *Destructive Emotions: How Can We Overcome Them?* New York: Bantam.

Hafen, B., K. Karren, K. Frandsen, and N. L. Smith. 1996. *Mind/Body Health.* Boston: Allyn and Bacon.

Halifax, J. 1993. *The Fruitful Darkness.* New York: HarperCollins.

Kabat-Zinn, J. 1982. An outpatient program in behavioral medicine for chronic pain patients based on the practice of mindfulness meditation: Theoretical considerations and preliminary results. *General Hospital Psychiatry* 4:33–47.

———. 1990. *Full Catastrophe Living.* New York: Delacorte Press.

Kabat-Zinn, J., A. Chapman, and P. Salmon. 1997. The relationship of cognitive and somatic components of anxiety to patient preference for alternative relaxation techniques. *Mind/Body Medicine* 2:101–09.

Kabat-Zinn, J., L. Lipworth, and R. Burney. 1985. The clinical use of mindfulness meditation for the self-regulation of chronic pain. *Journal of Behavioral Medicine* 8:163–90.

Kabat-Zinn, J., L. Lipworth, R. Burney, and W. Sellers. 1986. Four-year follow-up of a meditation-based program for the self-regulation of chronic pain: Treatment outcomes and compliance. *Clinical Journal of Pain* 2:159–73.

Kabat-Zinn, J., A. O. Massion, J. Kristeller, L. G. Peterson, K. E. Fletcher, L. Pbert, W. R. Lenderking, and S. F. Santorelli. 1992. Effectiveness of a meditation-based stress reduction program in the treatment of anxiety disorders. *American Journal of Psychiatry* 149:936–43.

Kabat-Zinn, J., E. Wheeler, T. Light, A. Skillings, M. Scharf, T. G. Cropley, D. Hosmer, and J. Bernhard. 1998. Influence of a mindfulness-based stress reduction intervention on rates of skin clearing in patients with moderate to severe psoriasis undergoing phototherapy (UVB) and photochemotherapy (PUVA). *Psychosomatic Medicine* 60:625–32.

Kaplan, K. H., D. L. Goldenberg, and M. Galvin-Nadeau. 1993. The impact of a meditation-based stress reduction program on fibromyalgia. *General Hospital Psychiatry* 15:284–89.

Kobasa, S. 1987. Stress responses and personality. In *Gender and Stress*, edited by R. Barnett, L. Biener, and G. Baruch. New York: Free Press.

———. 1990. Stress-resistant personality. In *The Healing Brain: A Scientific Reader*, edited by C. Swencionis and R. Ornstein. New York: Guilford.

Kornfield, J. 1993. *A Path with Heart.* New York: Bantam.

Kristeller, J. L., and C. B. Hallett. 1999. An exploratory study of a meditation-based intervention for binge-eating disorder. *Journal of Health Psychology* 4:357–63.

Langer, E. 1989. *Mindfulness.* Reading, Mass.: Perseus Press.

LeDoux, J. 1996. *The Emotional Brain.* New York: Touchstone.

Lepine, J. 2002. The epidemiology of anxiety disorders: Prevalence and social costs. *Journal of Clinical Psychiatry* 63 suppl 14:4–8.

Linehan, M. M. 1993a. *Cognitive-Behavioral Treatment of Borderline Personality Disorder.* New York: Guilford Press.

———. 1993b. *Skills Training Manual for Treating Borderline Personality Disorder.* New York: Guilford Press.

Miller, J. J., K. Fletcher, and J. Kabat-Zinn. 1995. Three-year follow-up and clinical implications of a mindfulness meditation-based stress reduction intervention in the treatment of anxiety disorders. *General Hospital Psychiatry* 17:192–200.

Moyers, B. 1993. *Healing and the Mind.* New York: Doubleday.

Perlmutter, C. 1993. Conquer chronic worry. *Prevention,* November, 75.

Ratey, J. 2001. *A User's Guide to the Brain.* New York: Vintage Books.

Roemer, L. 2002. Expanding our conceptualization of and treatment for generalized anxiety disorder: Integrating mindfulness/acceptance-based approaches with existing cognitive behavioral models. *Clinical Psychology: Science and Practice* 9:54–68.

Rosenberg, L., with D. Guy. 1998. *Breath by Breath.* Boston: Shambhala.

Roth, B. 1997. Mindfulness-based stress reduction in the inner city. *Advances 1997* 13:50–58.

Salzberg, S. 1995. *Loving-Kindness: The Revolutionary Art of Happiness.* Boston: Shambhala.

Shapiro, S. L., G. E. Schwartz, and G. Bonner. 1998. Effects of mindfulness-based stress reduction on medical and premedical students. *Journal of Behavioral Medicine* 21:581–97.

Speca, M., L. E. Carlson, E. Goodey, and M. Angen. 2000. A randomized, wait-list controlled clinical trial: The effect of a mindfulness meditation–based stress reduction program on mood and symptoms of stress in cancer outpatients. *Psychosomatic Medicine* 62:613–22.

Tarrant, J. 1998. *The Light inside the Dark.* New York: HarperCollins.

Taylor, S. 2002. *The Tending Instinct.* New York: Henry Holt.

Teasdale, J. D., Z. V. Segal, J. M. G. Williams, V. A. Ridgeway, J. M. Soulsby, and M. A. Lau. 2000. Prevention of relapse/recurrence in major depression by mindfulness-based cognitive therapy. *Journal of Consulting and Clinical Psychology* 68:615–23.

Thich Nhat Hanh. 1987. *Being Peace.* Berkeley, Calif.: Parallax Press.

Williams, R., and V. Williams. 1993. *Anger Kills.* New York: HarperCollins.

Wilson, R. R. 1986. *Don't Panic.* New York: Harper.

Jeffrey Brantley, MD, is a consulting associate in the Duke Department of Psychiatry and the founder and director of the Mindfulness-Based Stress Reduction Program at Duke University's Center for Integrative Medicine. He has also done multiple radio, television, and print media interviews regarding the MBSR program at Duke.

Jon Kabat-Zinn, Ph.D., is professor of medicine, emeritus, at the University of Massachusetts Medical School, founder and former director of its Stress Reduction Clinic, and founding executive director of its Center for Mindfulness in Medicine, Health Care, and Society. He is also the author of *Full Catastrophe Living* and *Wherever You Go, There You Are.*

Some Other
New Harbinger Titles

Your Surviving Spirit, Item 3570 $18.95

Coping with Anxiety, Item 3201 $10.95

The Agoraphobia Workbook, Item 3236 $19.95

Loving the Self-Absorbed, Item 3546 $14.95

Transforming Anger, Item 352X $10.95

Don't Let Your Emotions Run Your Life, Item 3090 $17.95

Why Can't I Ever Be Good Enough, Item 3147 $13.95

Your Depression Map, Item 3007 $19.95

Successful Problem Solving, Item 3023 $17.95

Working with the Self-Absorbed, Item 2922 $14.95

The Procrastination Workbook, Item 2957 $17.95

Coping with Uncertainty, Item 2965 $11.95

The BDD Workbook, Item 2930 $18.95

You, Your Relationship, and Your ADD, Item 299X $17.95

The Stop Walking on Eggshells Workbook, Item 2760 $18.95

Conquer Your Critical Inner Voice, Item 2876 $15.95

The PTSD Workbook, Item 2825 $17.95

Hypnotize Yourself Out of Pain Now!, Item 2809 $14.95

The Depression Workbook, 2nd edition, Item 268X $19.95

Beating the Senior Blues, Item 2728 $17.95

Shared Confinement, Item 2663 $15.95

Handbook of Clinical Psychopharmacology for Therpists, 3rd edition, Item 2698 $55.95

Call **toll free, 1-800-748-6273,** or log on to our online bookstore at **www.newharbinger.com** to order. Have your Visa or Mastercard number ready. Or send a check for the titles you want to New Harbinger Publications, Inc., 5674 Shattuck Ave., Oakland, CA 94609. Include $4.50 for the first book and 75¢ for each additional book, to cover shipping and handling. (California residents please include appropriate sales tax.) Allow two to five weeks for delivery.

Prices subject to change without notice.